Captivate, Activate,
and Invigorate
the
Student Brain
in Science and Math
Grades 6–12

*To Tessa: May your science and math teachers captivate,
activate, and invigorate your brain.*

—Dad

*I dedicate this book to my family, who have always been there for me
and continually encourage me to pursue my dreams. Smiles!*

—Ann M. Miller

Captivate, Activate, and Invigorate
the
Student Brain
in Science and Math
Grades 6–12

John Almarode
Ann M. Miller

CORWIN
A SAGE Company

CORWIN
A SAGE Company

FOR INFORMATION:

Corwin
A SAGE Company
2455 Teller Road
Thousand Oaks, California 91320
(800) 233-9936
www.corwin.com

SAGE Publications Ltd.
1 Oliver's Yard
55 City Road
London EC1Y 1SP
United Kingdom

SAGE Publications India Pvt. Ltd.
B 1/I 1 Mohan Cooperative Industrial Area
Mathura Road, New Delhi 110 044
India

SAGE Publications Asia-Pacific Pte. Ltd.
3 Church Street
#10-04 Samsung Hub
Singapore 049483

Printed in the United States of America.

A catalog record of this book is available from the Library of Congress.

ISBN: 9781452218021

This book is printed on acid-free paper.

Acquisitions Editor: Jessica Allan
Associate Editor: Kimberly Greenberg
Editorial Assistant: Heidi Arndt
Permissions Editor: Karen Ehrmann
Project Editor: Veronica Stapleton
Copy Editor: Diana Breti
Typesetter: C&M Digitals (P) Ltd.
Proofreader: Wendy Jo Dymond
Indexer: Sheila Bodell
Cover Designer: Anupama Krishnan

SUSTAINABLE FORESTRY INITIATIVE
Certified Chain of Custody
Promoting Sustainable Forestry
www.sfiprogram.org
SFI-01268
SFI label applies to text stock

13 14 15 16 17 10 9 8 7 6 5 4 3 2 1

Contents

Foreword

The past three decades have seen an explosion of information from the fields of cognitive science, neuroscience, and educational research. We've learned more in these few years than in all of history. Although everyone seems to be fascinated with these new findings, educators are perhaps more captivated than most. The reason is not difficult to understand: The brain is the organ of learning, but we have had little information about how it works! Our students' brains have been black boxes, with their secrets locked inside. Why is it that some children learn to read easily and others suffer great difficulty with the task? How is it a teacher can explain something one day and the next day students act as if they've never heard it? What role does emotion play in learning? How can teachers motivate reluctant learners?

Teaching involves making thousands of decisions each day; however, the knowledge base from which they've generated their decisions has been limited. Educational practice has been largely based on what the behavioral sciences could provide, which is sometimes helpful but not sufficient. There's more to teaching and learning than reinforcement theory. Of necessity we've operated intuitively. Intuition has worked well in many instances but has left us without the ability to articulate our craft to others. Because of this, we've become, as educator and expert on the brain Bob Sylwester puts it, a "folklore profession." This lack of scientific knowledge has left us at a disadvantage in designing pedagogy and implementing curriculum in our schools.

While neuroscientists seldom give educators specific suggestions on how to implement their findings in classrooms, the research is giving the field a new understanding of how the brain encodes, manipulates, and stores information, in other words, how it learns.

The bottom line is that the better we understand the human brain, the better we'll be able to make more informed decisions about how to teach it.

In this book, educators John Almarode and Ann Miller have made excellent strides in translating the research to practice. They synthesize research findings and theoretical frameworks about teaching and learning to give us a broad-based look at how educators might better engage students in meaningful learning. Almarode and Miller understand that without active engagement, learning is often rote and information is seldom retained. Using cleverly designed and motivating strategies, they provide numerous examples of how to actively involve students and make the curriculum at every grade level truly brain compatible.

Our students will be the ultimate beneficiaries of this user-friendly book that deserves to be on the desk of every teacher.

Pat Wolfe

Preface

The primary finding is this, student time spent engaged in relevant content appears to be an essential variable for which there is no substitute . . . Teachers who make a difference in students' achievement are those who put students in contact with curriculum materials and find ways to keep them in contact. (Rosenshine & Berliner, 1978, p. 12)

With the recent media attention focused on American students' performance in science and mathematics relative to the rest of the world, science and mathematics achievement in the United States has become a hot topic in education circles and public conversation (National Academy of Science, 2005, 2010; National Center for Educational Statistics, 2011a, 2011b; National Research Council, 2011; National Science Board 2007, 2008, 2010). After listening to the reports about America's science and mathematics students, the message that most of the public walks away with is that our students are falling behind. For every person involved in this discussion, there is an opinion on how to address the concern. Some argue that we need higher standards, while some argue for more funding, teacher preparation, or even the restructuring of public schools. As a response to yet another approach, Diane Ravitch (2011) stated, "We can't fire our way to excellence," which counters the desire of some stakeholders to simply fire teachers in low-performing classrooms.

The framework presented in this book takes a significantly different approach—an approach that is a ground-up framework. The best way to tackle a problem is to start with the things that are within your control. Sitting around dissecting the American Education

System leads to a time-consuming conversation that, in the end, solves nothing. Speaking in generalities such as America's students cannot do fractions, think critically, or avoid science and mathematics is purely venting and concludes without a solution. However, this is not the case in your classroom. Your classroom is where daily change can and does happen. The recipe for engagement takes the most recent understanding of how the student brain works and interfaces it with an approach for teaching science and mathematics. The end result is an engaging science and mathematics classroom for a wide range of diverse learners. As students file into our classrooms, it would be very difficult to anticipate or hypothesize about their expectations for the semester or the year. Students take classes for a variety of reasons. Whether students take our classes because biology and geometry are the next courses in the sequence, chemistry and trigonometry are requirements to graduate or they have room for an elective and picked physics and calculus to fill up their schedule influences what they expect from you and your class. However, our expectation should be that each and every student walks through the door at the beginning of class and out of the door at the end of class better off because he or she spent some time with us. This starts by designing each individual activity, lesson, conceptual unit, and science and mathematics course with the sole purpose of engaging the student brain.

So what would this look like? My guess is that every teacher would be interested in having every student fully engaged in learning from the start of class until the end of class. Would you be interested in picking up strategies that increased the levels of student engagement in your science or mathematics classroom? Would you be interested in a list of "must-haves" for increasing student engagement? That is exactly what this book sets out to provide a framework for captivating, activating, and invigorating your students, keeping them engaged in your science and mathematics classroom. This book presents a list of six essential ingredients for cooking up an engaging science and mathematics classroom. In the form of a recipe, these six ingredients are based on the latest research brought to you by neuroscientists, cognitive scientists, and educational psychologists, synthesized and summarized for classroom application. If you stir and blend these ingredients with the strategies that you are currently using in your classroom, you will take your students' learning to a new level. This book highlights the relevant application of the research findings to your instructional lessons.

Important Features of the Book

This book not only provides a recipe for engaging the student brain in science and mathematics; it also strives to model the very ideas presented in each chapter. To reinforce each ingredient and promote the transfer of ideas from this book to your classroom, several in-text features are included:

- Stop-n-Thinks to break the information up into chunks and provide opportunities to review, revise, and process the information
- Exit Tickets to consolidate information and bring closure to the big ideas or concepts presented in each chapter
- Engaging Professional Development Tasks that promote the application of the big ideas or concepts to your classroom while at the same time encouraging collaboration between you and your colleagues
- Metaphors and Analogies provide references to concrete objects, events, or topics that promote clarity and understanding of abstract ideas or concepts presented in the chapter (e.g., the hippocampus acts as a surge protector for the brain)

The important features of the book reinforce each ingredient and promote the transfer of ideas by modeling them. Although the Stopn-Thinks, Exit Tickets, Engaging Professional Development Tasks, and the metaphors and analogies are targeted at you, each of these features can be modified and used in your science and mathematics classroom.

This brings up the final and most important feature of the book: strategies. Each chapter is stuffed full of strategies that highlight the ingredients of the engagement recipe. These strategies are examples and can be applied to your classroom as is or be tweaked to better fit your unique environment. Furthermore, many of the strategies apply across several ingredients. We have worked hard to provide a range of strategies across the variety of science and mathematics classes found in a typical middle or high school. Our hope is that this book will engage your brain to take the strategies presented in this book and adjust them to work in your classroom.

Breakdown of Chapters

In the chapters that follow, we present each ingredient of the recipe, the brain science behind it, and ready-to-use strategies and examples that make each ingredient classroom ready. Before we dive into the recipe, we have to get familiar with the elements of engagement. What we are talking about here is the student brain! If we are going make a deliberate effort to engage the brains of our students, it is helpful to understand how the student brain works, at least in terms of how it engages in learning. Chapter 2 builds background knowledge and familiarize you with the parts of the brain that are implicated in attention, engagement, and learning.

Chapter 3 presents the importance of priming the brain and the role of prior knowledge in new learning. Chapter 4 presents amazing research on the use of novelty to grab students' attention and enable them to remember what they are paying attention to.

Pause for a moment and call up those feelings that surface when a student has just asked, "Why do we have to know this?" or "Is this going to be on the test?" These questions are sure signs that your students are seeking relevance. That is the topic of Chapter 5. Chapters 6 and 7 look at the input and attentional limitations of the brain and how information moves from short-term to long-term memory. Finally, Chapter 8 pulls it all together by helping you develop an action plan for implementing the ideas you came up with throughout the book.

References

National Academy of Science. (2005). *Rising above the gathering storm: Energizing and employing America for a brighter economic future.* Washington, DC: National Academies Press.

National Academy of Science. (2010). *Rising above the gathering storm, revisited: Rapidly approaching category 5.* Washington, DC: National Academies Press.

National Center for Education Statistics. (2011a). *The nation's report card: Science 2009* (NCES 2011-451). Washington, DC: Institute of Education Sciences, U.S. Department of Education. Retrieved February 1, 2011, from http://nces.ed.gov/nationsreportcard/pubs/main2009/2011451.asp

National Center for Education Statistics. (2011b). *The nation's report card: Trial urban district assessment mathematics 2011* (NCES 2012-452). Washington, DC: Institute of Education Sciences, U.S. Department of Education.

National Research Council. (2011). *A framework for K–12 science education: Practices, crosscutting concepts, and core ideas.* Committee on a Conceptual Framework for the New K–12 Science Education Standards. Board on Science Education, Division of Behavioral and Social Sciences in Education. Washington, DC: The National Academies Press.

National Science Board. (2007). *National action plan for addressing the critical needs of the U.S. science, technology, engineering, and mathematics education system.* Arlington, VA: National Science Foundation.

National Science Board. (2008). *Science and engineering indicators 2008* (Vol. 1, NSB 08-01; Vol. 2, NSB 08-01A). Arlington, VA: National Science Foundation.

National Science Board. (2010). *Science and engineering indicators 2010* (NSB 10-01). Arlington, VA: National Science Foundation.

Ravitch, D. (2011). Second response from Diane Ravitch. *Eduwonk.com.* Retrieved from http://www.eduwonk.com/2011/11/second-response-from-diane-ravitch.html

Rosenshine, B., & Berliner, D. C. (1978). Academic engaged time. *British Journal of Teacher Education, 4,* 3–16.

Acknowledgments

C *aptivate, Activate, and Invigorate* was a feat not accomplished alone. For this reason, I wish to thank several very important people for the never-ending encouragement and support they provided to me during this project.

Thank you Ann for joining me on this project. Your contributions reflect the incredible wealth of information you possess on effective teaching and learning. I am honored to have you as a colleague and, more important, a friend.

I want to both acknowledge and thank the members of the Corwin team: Jessica Allan, Kimberly Greenbert, Heidi Arndt, Karen Ehrmann, Veronica Hooper, Diana Breti, and Anupama Krishnan. Your time, effort, and feedback during this entire process have been incredible. I am forever grateful for your expertise in taking this manuscript from initial draft to its published form.

Please allow me share the story about the development of my interest in the brain and learning. In 2004, I began working on my master's degree. In my curriculum and instruction class, one of the recommended readings (recommended, not required) was the book *Brain Matters: Translating Research Into Classroom Practice* by Patricia Wolfe. I was confused and skeptical. Why would a book about the brain even be on the recommended reading list for a curriculum and instruction class? As a confused skeptic, I ordered the book and started reading it. I read it cover to cover in less than three days. It made perfect sense and I was hooked. Jump ahead eight years to the professional development day for Twin Rivers R10 School District in rural Missouri. I am about 10 minutes away from starting an all-day workshop with one half of the district's faculty. The next day, I would work with the other half of the district's faculty. As I prepare to get started, a very elegant and stately looking woman taps me on the shoulder. I turn around and nothing could have prepared me for what I was about to see or hear: "Good morning, I am Pat Wolfe." I had crossed paths with the woman whose book sparked my interest in the brain and learning. Although she never knew it until that day in Missouri, she has been an inspiration to me for almost a decade. For that alone, Pat, I am forever thankful.

My interest in the brain and learning led me to attend a six-day workshop facilitated by Eric Jensen. I was hungry to learn more, and he has a lot of knowledge to share. The six days I spent with Eric Jensen that summer were life changing. His depth of knowledge and delivery of content is something to behold. The next three years flew by as I attended each of his workshops and earned a spot on his certified trainers list. I have Eric Jensen to thank for getting me started as a professional developer. Eric has been incredibly supportive and encouraging in all aspects of my professional career. His work ethic and drive for excellence is inspiring and motivating. I am grateful to have him as a colleague, mentor, and friend. Thank you, Eric.

Now, on to my teachers. I believe my interest in science and mathematics can be attributed to the fabulous science and math teachers whose classes I had the privilege of attending from sixth grade to twelfth grade: Sally Cross, Diann Snyder, Ellen Clouse, Deborah McCormick, David Wade, Ken Patterson, Len Klein, Thomas O'Neill, Ann Higgins, Richard Showalter, Francis Harouff, Terry Wampler, Betsy Painter, Sam Alexander, Kathy Garber, and Ray Lee. These folks are true masters in their profession and are responsible for a large part of who I am today.

In addition to being my teachers, Sally Cross and Diann Snyder changed my life. The actions of these two women are the reasons I became a science and math teacher. As my sixth-grade science teacher, Sally Cross served as my first example of a "real" science teacher. The level of emotional, behavioral, and cognitive engagement that she fostered and nurtured in Room 30 at Stuarts Draft Middle School left an indelible mark on me. Diann Snyder has been part of my life since my days in diapers. She found the spark I had for science and ignited the flame into what became a passion for science and mathematics. These two women continue to be a guiding light in my career as a teacher educator at James Madison University. Classrooms and students need more Ms. Crosses and Ms. Snyders. I can honestly say that I would not be who I am or be doing what I do if it were not for Sally Cross and Diann Snyder. These words are not enough, but they are the only option for this page. Thank you.

I want to say thank you to my former students at Stuarts Draft High School and the Shenandoah Valley Governor's School. Thank you for making my job as a teacher the greatest job on earth. Thank you to the thousands of teachers that I have had the pleasure of working with in professional development settings.

The first teachers in my life were my parents, Jim and Elaine Almarode, and my younger brother, Joe. They have always offered unyielding support and belief in the choices I have made in my life. Whether I was dissecting a pig in the basement or insisting on a real chemistry set, they were supportive. Their approach to life will forever inspire me to achieve.

I have saved the most important acknowledgment for last. My wife, Danielle Taylor Almarode, has had front-row seats to this entire process. The sacrifices she has made and the amazing support she has provided have not gone unnoticed. Her personal dedication to my success is admirable and leaves me in awe. I will forever be indebted to her and look forward to a lifetime of "returning the favor."

John Almarode

My sincere gratitude goes to my coauthor, John Almarode, who invited me to join him on this journey and continually encouraged and inspired me along the way. I think we make a great team.

The success of this book would not have been possible without the support of my loving husband. He has always been incredibly supportive of my professional goals, and for that I am extremely grateful. There are no words that could truly express the appreciation and love in my heart for my mom and dad. I would not be where I am today without the strong, loving foundation they provided for me as a child. Much of what I have learned during my life is a result of being a mom to three remarkable and delightful children, all of whom I love so dearly. Thank you, kids!

Most educators can think of that one special educational leader who made a lasting difference in their lives. For me, that person was Mrs. Rebecca Kaune. It is due to her teaching, guidance, and determination never to give up on me that I enjoy the career I have today. She continues to inspire my thoughts and actions. So to her, I am eternally grateful.

Thank you to all the readers who are willing to actively explore and implement the content and strategies in this book. I am confident that your students will thank you, too.

Above all, I thank God for all the blessings and good fortune in my life.

Ann Miller

Publisher's Acknowledgments

Corwin wishes to acknowledge the following peer reviewers for their editorial insight and guidance:

JoAnn Hiatt
Mathematics teacher
Olathe East High School
Olathe, KS

Loukea N. Kovanis-Wilson
Chemistry Instructor
Clarkston High School
Clarkston, MI

Rosalind LaRocque
Professional Development Coordinator
American Federation of Teachers
Washington, DC

Amanda P. McKee
Algebra Instructor
Johnsonville High School
Johnsonville, SC

Melissa Miller
Middle School Science Instructor
Lynch Middle School
Farmington, AR

Edward C. Nolan
PreK–12 Content Specialist, Mathematics
Montgomery County Public Schools
Rockville, Maryland

Patricia Waller
Educational Consultant and Retired Science Educator
Emmaus High School
Emmaus, PA

Marian White-Hood
Director of Academics
Maya Angelou Public Charter School & SeeForever Foundation
Washington, DC

About the Authors

Dr. John Almarode, an educator and staff developer for many years, has worked with all age groups in education, from prekindergarteners to graduate students. John began his career in Augusta County, Virginia teaching a wide range of students. He then taught Pre-Calculus, Physics, and Modern Physics at the Shenandoah Valley Governor's School for three years. While at the Governor's School, a significant proportion his time was devoted to providing outreach and enrichment activities to preK through eighth-grade students. As a staff developer, John has presented locally, regionally, nationally, and internationally. He has worked with thousands of teachers, dozens of school districts, and multiple organizations. John's action-packed workshops offer participants ready-to-use strategies and the brain rules that make them work. John is a faculty member of the College of Education at James Madison University, where he works with preservice teachers and inservice teachers and pursues his research interests in how to engage all students. He lives in Waynesboro, Virginia, with his wife Danielle, a fellow educator; their daughter Tessa; and their two dogs, Angel and Forest.

Ann M. Miller is currently the K–12 Coordinator of Professional Development and Elementary Instruction for Waynesboro Public Schools. Ann has a strong teaching and leadership background. She received her undergraduate and master's degrees from the State University of Oswego in New York before completing her Certification of Administration from the State University of New York in Cortland. Ann dedicated most of her teaching career to special education students, focusing on emotionally disturbed students, before making a successful transition to the position of Instructional Specialist. Ann became a member of an elite team of staff development leaders in which her enthusiasm and approachable style help to develop strong, productive learning communities in their nine component districts.

Over the years, Ann's firm belief in staying on the cutting edge of instructional strategies encouraged her to study differentiated instruction, cooperative learning, Baldrige quality tools, classroom instruction that works, mentoring, win–win discipline, and essential elements of instruction. Although these are just a few areas of study, this wealth of knowledge has provided the strong instructional foundation needed to design and present relevant and meaningful learning opportunities. She understands the challenges of education and is committed to the implementation of quality staff development programs that promote student achievement as well as the recruitment and retention of quality teachers and school administrators.

1

The Recipe for an Engaged Brain

Every weekday morning without fail, we climb out of bed, after striking the snooze button on the alarm clock the maximum allowable number of times, and prepare ourselves for an often unpredictable, but ultimately rewarding, day as an elite group of professionals dedicated to the development and achievement of all students. We are teachers. Our important and carefully scripted morning routine serves as a necessary process to ready ourselves for the action-packed day of "reading, writing, and arithmetic." Reading teachers are revving up for a day of context clues, inferences, and reading comprehension. For writing teachers, distinguishing between active and passive voice may be on the agenda. Physical education teachers, music teachers, and art teachers prepare to construct classroom experiences that promote wellness and creative expression. As mathematics and science teachers, we passionately prepare to pass along the great ideas of algebra, geometry, earth science, physics, and biology just as the intellectual giants of our disciplines, like Euclid, Pythagoras, Newton, and Einstein, did many years ago. Math teachers may battle the challenge of improper fractions, solving equations, or completing the square, all while spearheading the fight against dependence on a calculator. Orchestrating an enriched laboratory activity that promotes and models the true nature of science and the knowledge derived from it is paramount just down the hall in the science wing.

Although the specifics of the day differ across grade levels, classrooms, and content areas, each teacher gambles on the willingness of students to "play along" and engage in his or her carefully crafted vision for the day. On the very best of days, students are eager, interested, and compliant from the beginning of the day until the final dismissal bell. They willingly complete all tasks and assignments handed to them, including those tasks and assignments reserved for "after hours." The students do their homework! The other end of the spectrum would be an apathetic, disinterested, and defiant student who notices each tick of the clock and agonizes over every second. Obviously, this student has no interest in completing any tasks or assignments, and we don't even think about collecting homework from him or her. Although individual levels of engagement fluctuate from day to day, class to class, and even minute to minute, most of you can visualize a number of students who fall on various locations along the engagement spectrum (see Figures 1.1 and 1.2). What does engagement look like and sound like?

Figure 1.1   Engaged Students

Figure 1.2   Disengaged Students

Stop-n-Think Box 1.1

If you were to look out over your classroom, how would you recognize a student who was engaged in your science or mathematics lesson? How would you recognize a student who was not engaged in your lesson?

- Make a list of behaviors and observable characteristics associated with a student engaged in your classroom.
- Make a second list of behaviors and observable characteristics associated with a student *not* engaged in your classroom.

The Recipe for Student Engagement

The recipe for student engagement contains six "must-have" ingredients and just as many steps. Grab your lab coat and protractor, gather a group of young science and math brains, and get ready.

Photo from Thinkstock.com.

1. **Prime** the brain. Stir.

2. Sprinkle in the right amount of **novelty**. Continue to stir.

3. Insert a good portion of **relevance**. Blend together with the content often.

4. Pour into the **big picture** and mix together some more.

5. **Marinate** for approximately 15 minutes; then stir once more.

6. Allow to cook for two to three days, **checking** often for degree of doneness. Stir as needed.

This recipe provides a framework for structuring your next lesson on the Krebs cycle (see Figure 1.3), Newton's Third Law of Motion (see Figure 1.4), salinity of the world's oceans (see Figure 1.5), the Pythagorean Theorem (see Figure 1.6), or solving systems of equations (see Figure 1.7).

This recipe also provides a framework for structuring your next unit on circuits, stoichiometry, quadratic equations, or linear inequalities. Taken individually, the ingredients likely will not result in the desired outcome: student engagement. After all, simply making learning novel without "checking for degree of doneness" does not do the student brain any favors, just like a teaspoon of salt is never as delectable by itself as it is in freshly baked chocolate chip cookies. The power of the end result happens when the ingredients are blended together. Together the ingredients create a classroom environment that will not only increase student engagement in the learning experience, but ultimately will also increase the level of student achievement in your classroom. In the chapters that follow, we will present each ingredient of the recipe, the brain science behind it, and ready-to-use strategies and examples that make each ingredient classroom ready.

Figure 1.3   Krebs Cycle

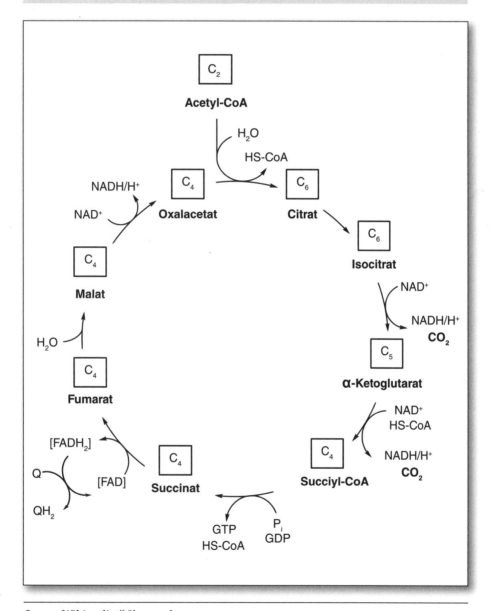

Source: Wikipedia/Yikrazuul.

Figure 1.4   Newton's Third Law of Motion

Photo from Thinkstock.com.

Figure 1.5   Salinity of the World's Oceans

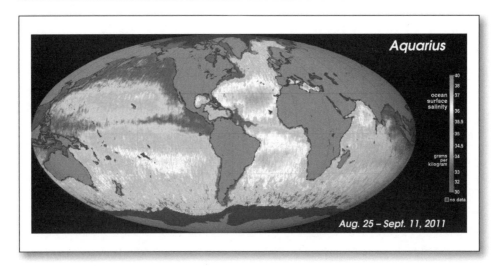

Source: NASA/GSFC/JPL-Caltech.

Figure 1.6   Pythagorean Theorem

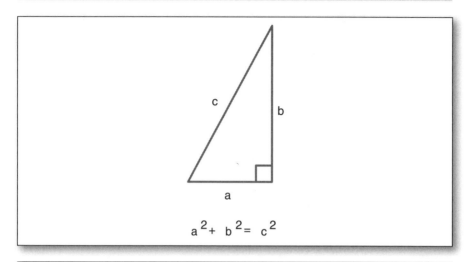

$$a^2 + b^2 = c^2$$

Source: Wikimedia.org.

Figure 1.7   Solving Systems of Equations

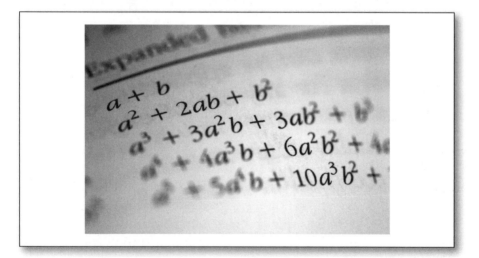

Photo from Thinkstock.com.

Recipes as Frameworks

Granny's kitchen was a simple but magical place. The head chef was a five-foot-tall woman of God who took unimaginable pride in her family, her housework, and her cooking. Until the day she died, her memory retrieval about the proper way to make butter, homemade bread, chicken and dumplings, and pie with a from-scratch piecrust was 100% accurate. Yet, if you were to ask her about the day's visitors to the nursing home, her recall was more like that of a 16-year-old taking a test in trigonometry the day before the homecoming dance: mediocre at best. However, the real point of this story has to do with my grandmother's use of recipes. She had a lot of them. They were organized by courses and then by main ingredients. But the keen observer would notice that she never used a recipe while in action. With more than 80 years of practice, she had mastered each dish and prepared it by relying only on her memory.

As her health began to decline, it was obvious to many of us in the family that Granny's kitchen traditions were at risk of being lost forever. In the interest of preserving such delectable heirlooms, I bravely asked for her recipes and gave them a try. To my amazement, they tasted nothing like Granny's. I followed them step by step, not deviating even a whisk, teaspoon, or degree from her original recipe. What could possibly have gone wrong? Not a single bite was as good as Granny's. Then it hit me: My grandmother used recipes as the framework. She then adjusted each step, depending on the other dishes or the hungry people who would slide their feet under her dinner table the moment these dishes were ready. A little more of this, a little less of that, and she managed, each time, to find perfection. It was then that I discovered she was an expert at the skill of monitoring and adjusting. These two skills also serve as the foundation for successful teachers.

The recipe for student engagement we present in this book is analagous to my grandmother's recipe for chicken and dumplings: The six "key ingredients" (prime, novelty, relevance, big picture, marinate, and checking) provide a framework for cooking up a highly engaged classroom and serving intrigued and successful students. However, the way you ration the ingredients in your classroom may be completely different from the way Mrs. Smith, two doors down, does it. Mrs. Smith's students may need more priming and less novelty, simply because the learning of the day is novel enough by itself (e.g., combustion reactions in chemistry, fractals in geometry, or tornados in earth science). You, on the other hand, may find that an extra pinch of relevance is exactly what your recipe needs that day. Not only will this differ from classroom to classroom, but the recipe may need adjusting from topic to topic and day to day.

Each student in your science or mathematics classroom has a grocery list of experiences, both positive and negative, that have had a profound influence on his or her brain. In addition, these experiences strongly influence student attitudes and dispositions toward science and mathematics. Given that no two individuals have the same experiences in life or in the classroom, differences among teenage brains are the norm, not the exception (Blakemore, 2012; Casey & Jones, 2010; Choudhury, 2010; Crawford, 2007; Feinstein, 2009; Powell, 2006; Schenck, 2011; Wolfe, 2010). Simply put, no two brains are alike. The factors that contribute to this diversity among brains include, and certainly are not limited to, genetics, relationships, socioeconomic status, and the environment (Anderson, Anderson, Northam, Jacobs, & Catroppa, 2001; Baydar, Brooks-Gunn, & Furstenberg, 1994; Blakemore, 2008; Chow & Stewart, 1972; Driemeyer, Boyke, Gaser, Buchel, & May, 2008; Gottfried, Gottfried, Bathurst, Guerin, & Parramore, 2003; Greenough, Black, & Wallace, 1987; Grossman, Churchill, Bates, Kleim, & Greenough, 2002; Huttenlocher, 1979; Maguire et al., 2000; McGivern, Andersen, Byrd, Mutter, & Reilly, 2002; Rutter & O'Conner, 2004; Sameroff, 1998; Weisel & Hubel, 1965; Yakovlev & Lecours, 1967). In fact, some researchers argue that genetics contributes approximately 30% of who we are as individuals; the rest is environment (Devlin, Daniels, & Roeder, 1997; Saudino, 2005). Therefore, a cookie-cutter approach to engagement is both unrealistic and inappropriate. Just as you would adjust the recipe for a home-cooked meal to taste, the recipe for engagement can be adjusted.

Addressing the individual needs of the wide range of learners who populate your science or mathematics class would take volumes, not chapters. However, modifying the recipe in this book can meet the needs of diverse learners in science and mathematics.

It is our belief that, over time, you will master the use of the recipe and simply adjust it according to the needs of the faces staring back at you as you assume your position at the front of the room. How will you know when to adjust the recipe?

Using Your Engagement Monitor

Stop-n-Think Box 1.2

No one knows your classroom better than you. Make a list of the big ideas or major concepts that you teach in a given month, semester, or year. Based on your past experiences, which of these ideas or concepts need more priming? More or less novelty? More or less relevance? Which ideas or concepts require more checking for degree of doneness?

Did you know that the average teacher typically makes about 1,500 decisions every day (A. Fredericks, 2005)? Many of these decisions concern the development and presentation of a well-cooked lesson. The monitoring and adjusting process starts with your content and relies on your experience in the classroom. As you monitor and observe the students' behaviors, you should be watching for those observable characteristics you previously identified in Stop-n-Think Box 1.1. Then ask yourself, are those behaviors telling you that little Johnny's brain is highly engaged, or are they simply telling you that his brain has "left the building"?

How often do you create 100% active participation—the continuous, ongoing, simultaneous engagement of all students in relevant learning—in your classroom? Wouldn't it be great if every time you asked a question or presented a task you generated 100% participation? It is possible!

Engagement: An Overt and Covert Operation

There are three types of engagement: behavioral engagement, emotional engagement, and cognitive engagement (Appleton, Christenson, & Furlong, 2008; J. Fredricks, Blumenfeld, & Paris, 2004; Reschly, Huebner, Appleton, & Antaramian, 2008; Skinner, Kinderman, & Furrer, 2009). In the classroom, on any given day the odometer readings for each individual student fluctuate across these three types of engagement (see Table 1.1).

Table 1.1   Three Types of Engagement

Type of Engagement	Description
Behavioral Engagement	The student is compliant with all rules, regulations, and instructions. Put differently, the student does exactly what he or she is supposed to do. This is the most easily observable type of engagement.
Emotional Engagement	The student is vested in the classroom, lesson, and/or activity. He or she has bought into what is happening in the classroom and thus feels connected to his or her learning. This is the most overlooked type of engagement.

Type of Engagement	Description
Cognitive Engagement	The student is thinking about what he or she is engaged in at this particular moment.
	Hands-on and minds-on.
	The occurrence of this type of engagement depends on the specific strategy, task, or activity provide by the teacher.

For example, students may shuffle in at 8:00 a.m. on time with all of their supplies (high behavioral engagement), but they may have no interest in being at school (low emotional engagement). Or, a student in the third row, second seat back has her book, notebook, pencil, and calculator out on her desk; she is sitting quietly while the teacher presents an example of how to graph a linear inequality in algebra or set up a free-body diagram in physics (high behavioral engagement). However, the student is daydreaming about this Friday's high school football game (low cognitive engagement).

Stop-n-Think Box 1.3

List specific examples of strategies that promote behavioral engagement, emotional engagement, and cognitive engagement.

The task for us as teachers is to cook up a plan that encourages all three types of engagement. A teacher who stresses behavioral engagement (e.g., lots of rules, procedures, and a superb classroom discipline system) will only be successful if he or she includes specific strategies to promote emotional and cognitive engagement. Otherwise, he or she will have a room full of well-behaved students who are miserable and thinking about all of the other places they would rather be. Similarly, if you have cognitively complex and engaging activities, but your classroom is a three-ringed circus, student achievement will suffer. The recipe for engagement is designed to provide a guide to finding the ideal balance of behavioral, emotional, and cognitive engagement by pairing research on the student brain with specific classroom strategies. These strategies come in two distinct forms: overt and covert.

You can increase the level of student engagement by making a conscious decision to use these two different strategies simultaneously.

Whenever your students' behavior can be observed, monitored, or measured, they are exhibiting an overt response (Corno, 1993; Finn, 1989, 1993; Finn & Voelkl, 1993; Pintrich, 2004; Schunk & Zimmerman, 2003; Vrugt & Oort, 2008). Quite often teachers successfully engage their students in many overt activities throughout the day, such as creating a nonlinguistic representation, engaging in a peer conversation, drafting an advanced organizer, or performing a demonstration. All of these activities can be observed, measured, or monitored by the teacher and by other students. There are also activities that cannot be seen, measured, or monitored: Whenever you ask your students to think, imagine, visualize, or go over something in their minds, you are asking them to perform a covert behavior (Appleton, Christenson, Kim, & Reschly, 2006; Corno, 1993; Finn, 1989, 1993; Finn & Voelkl, 1993; Furlong & Christenson, 2008; Pintrich, 2004; Schunk & Zimmerman, 2003; Vrugt & Oort, 2008). Even though you cannot observe, hear, measure, or monitor the activity, if the students are performing the requested task, it is active participation.

Much of the thinking done in formal education has focused on skills of analysis. As students perform many of the 21st-century learning skills, they will be engaging in a covert activity. This includes mentally estimating answers, identifying and eliminating incorrect responses, and critically thinking about logical solutions. When we request these tasks, we are creating covert learning experiences for our students. Developing the thinking skills of your students is becoming a vital part of education. When they go out in the working world, potential employers will be seeking employees who are proficient at exploring ideas, generating possibilities, and seeking multiple answers to challenges. This is only one reason why it is essential that teachers make conscious decisions to embed both overt and covert active participation in their lessons.

The real bang for your planning buck will come when you combine these two strategies. When the strategies are used separately, the students you intentionally involve in an overt activity (e.g., putting a problem on the board, explaining a particular concept, or answering a question) are highly engaged; however, too often this leaves the rest of the students in the class disinterested and unengaged. Consequently, teachers are often occupied with the students who are engaged and don't even realize that a large percentage of the students are waiting or tuning out. Put yourself in their shoes. If a teacher calls on a student to describe the difference between abiotic and biotic factors in an ecosystem, in most cases, his or her classmates are either relieved because they were not called on or are disappointed that they were not allowed to show off their knowledge of ecosystems. In both cases, the odds of them checking out for this time are probably quite high. So the next time you ask a student, or several students, to go up to the interactive whiteboard to complete an equation or solve a problem, simultaneously assign a covert thinking activity to the other students in the room. If a student is sharing his or her solution of a physics or chemistry problem, ask the other students to check their solutions, step by step, looking for alternative routes or areas where they would have done something different. What a great opportunity to stimulate higher-level thinking, embed creative thought, or develop problem-solving skills. It can be as simple as asking the other students to reflect on the process the student used to derive the solution or to develop a different method for finding the solution and then explain their thoughts.

Stop-n-Think Box 1.4

What are other strategies for fostering overt engagement in your science or math classroom? What are some ideas you have for simultaneously combining overt and covert strategies?

You Can Lead Students to Class, but Can You Make Them Think?

Many teachers will argue that you cannot make students think. They are exactly right! If we create a climate in which one or two students volunteer to participate, the others may disengage or feel no accountability for participating. Instead, create an engaging climate by inviting your students to think, and then follow up by giving them the opportunity to show and tell you what, in fact, they thought about. For example, two very important words can make a huge difference: *all* and *everybody* (see Table 1.2).

It is amazing how those two simple words, *all* and *everyone* can increase the level of active participation. Try it; you'll like it! Set the expectation that all your students will think, instead of unintentionally sending the message that whoever wants to participate is welcome to share his or her thoughts. When you expect students to think and participate, you are requiring that students put forth effort. Once you have made the conscious decisions necessary to result in a certain percentage of your students engaging in an overt activity and the

Table 1.2 Volunteering Versus Engaging

Volunteering Climate	Engaging Climate
Who would like to . . .?	Everybody, be ready to . . .
Would someone please read . . .?	All of you think about a method that will . . .
Can anyone tell me why . . .?	Everyone write down . . . and raise your hand when you are ready to share.

remainder of your students engaging in some type of covert thought process, you have created the expectation that all of your students are engaged. Congratulations, you are on your way to 100% active participation!

As a note for emphasis, this usually does not *just happen.* During the planning process, as you develop your lessons you will need to make conscious decisions to embed the different types of engagement within the recipe. Active participation has been known to increase students' rate and degree of learning, create motivation, and help students develop those relevant meaningful connections that are so important for the brain (Connell, Spencer, & Aber, 1994; Marks, 2000; Pashler, 1999; Skinner, Wellborn, & Connell, 1990; Styles, 1997).

CHAPTER 1: 3-2-1 EXIT TICKET

List at least **three** ideas or concepts you want to remember from this chapter.

Photo from
Thinkstock.com.

Describe at least **two** strategies you will take away from this chapter and try out in your classroom.

What is **one** challenge you will face as you implement the ideas from this chapter?

Engaging Professional Development Tasks

1. This professional development task involves a video critique of your teaching. Video record yourself teaching a lesson or activity. Set up the flip camera or digital video recorder so that when you review the digital recording, you can see the behavior of the students in your classroom and your behaviors as a teacher. Wait a day or two and watch your teaching video by yourself to ensure an honest evaluation and critique. Make notes of what you observe during this teaching episode. Use the following questions to guide your reflection about your teaching video:

   • Are your students engaged? How many are and how many are not?
   • What are you using as evidence to decide whether they are or are not engaged?

- Can you identify the use of covert and overt engagement strategies?
- Is your climate a volunteering climate or an engaging climate?
- What are your students doing while you are teaching?
- Does the level of student engagement change during the lesson or activity? Is this change associated with a particular part of the lesson or activity?
- How has this video review and reflection changed your perspective on your teaching and student engagement?

2. This professional development task focuses on the use of the recipe to increase engagement in a diverse classroom. No two students are alike. In your classroom, students come from diverse socioeconomic, ethnic, racial, and cultural backgrounds. Similarly, students vary across a range of cognitive ability, learner readiness, and interest levels. As a result, the recipe for engagement must be seasoned to taste. That is, the amount of time spent on any one part of the recipe should be directly related to the characteristics of the students in the class. How might the recipe be modified for the following students?

- A student with attention-deficit/hyperactivity disorder, dyslexia, or another learning disability.
- A student who comes from a low socioeconomic status.
- A student whose primary language is not English.
- A student who is highly gifted in science and mathematics or has parents in science- and mathematics-related disciplines.

What parts of the recipe may need more emphasis or less emphasis? Why do you believe that to be the case?

References

Anderson, V., Anderson, P., Northam, E., Jacobs, R., & Catroppa, C. (2001). Development of executive functions through late childhood and adolescence in an Australian sample. *Developmental Neuropsychology, 20*, 385–406.

Appleton, J., Christenson, S., & Furlong, M. (2008). Student engagement with school: Critical conceptual and methodological issues of the construct. *Psychology in the Schools, 45*, 369–386.

Appleton, J., Christenson, S., Kim, D., & Reschly, A. (2006). Measuring cognitive and psychological engagement: Validation of the Student Engagement Instrument. *Journal of School Psychology, 44*, 427–445.

Baydar, N., Brooks-Gunn, J., & Furstenberg, F. (1993). Early warning signs of functional illiteracy. Predictors in childhood and adolescence. *Child Development, 64*(3), 815–829.

Blakemore, S. J. (2008). The social brain in adolescence. *Nature Reviews Neuroscience, 9,* 267–277.

Blakemore, S. J. (2012). Imaging brain development: The adolescent brain. *NeuroImage, 61*(2), 397–406.

Casey, B. J., & Jones, R. M. (2010). Neurobiology of the adolescent brain and behavior: implications for substance use disorders. *Journal of the American Academy of Child and Adolescent Psychiatry, 49,* 1189–1201.

Choudhury, S. (2010). Culturing the adolescent brain: What can neuroscience learn from anthropology? *Social Cognitive Affective Neuroscience, 5*(2–3), 159–167.

Chow, K. L., & Stewart, D. L. (1972). Reversal of structural and functional effects of long-term visual deprivation in cats. *Experimental Neurology, 34,* 409–433.

Connell, J. P., Spencer, M. B., & Aber, J. L. (1994). Educational risk and resilience in African-American youth: Context, self, action, and outcomes in school. *Child Development, 65,* 493–506.

Corno, L. (1993). The best-laid plans: Modern conceptions of volition and educational research. *Educational Researcher, 22*(2), 14–22.

Crawford, G. B. (2007). *Brain-based teaching with adolescent learning in mind* (2nd ed.). Thousand Oaks, CA: Corwin.

Devlin, B., Daniels, M., & Roeder, K. (1997). The heritability of IQ. *Nature, 388*(6641), 468–471.

Driemeyer, J., Boyke, J., Gaser, C., Buchel, C., & May, A. (2008). Changes in gray matter induced by learning—Revisited. *PLoS ONE, 3*(7), e2669.

Feinstein, S. G. (2009). *Secrets of the teenage brain: Research-based strategies for reaching and teaching today's adolescents* (2nd ed.). Thousand Oaks, CA: Corwin.

Finn, J. (1989). Withdrawing from school. *Review of Educational Research, 59,* 117–142.

Finn, J. (1993). *School engagement and students at risk.* Washington, DC: National Center for Educational Statistics.

Finn, J., & Voelkl, K. (1993). School characteristics related to school engagement. *The Journal of Negro Education, 62,* 249–268.

Fredericks, A. D. (2005). *The complete idiot's guide to success as a teacher.* New York: Penguin Group.

Fredericks, J. A., Blumenfeld, P. C., & Paris, A. H. (2004). School engagement: Potential of the concept, state of the evidence. *Review of Educational Research, 74*(1), 49–109.

Furlong, M. J., & Christenson, S. L. (2008). Engaging students at school and with learning: A relevant construct for all students. *Psychology in Schools, 45*(5), 365–368.

Gottfried, A. W., Gottfried, A. E., Bathurst, K., Guerin, D. W., & Parramore, M. M. (2003). Socioeconomic status in children's development and family environment: Infancy through adolescence. In M. H. Bornstein & R. H. Bradley (Eds.), *Socioeconomic status, parenting, and child development* (pp. 260–285). Mahwah, NJ: Lawrence Erlbaum Associates.

Greenough, W. T., Black, J. E., & Wallace, C. S. (1987). Experience and brain development. *Child Development, 58,* 539–559.

Grossman, A. W., Churchill, J. D., Bates, K. E., Kleim, J. A., & Greenough, W. T. (2002). A brain adaptation view of plasticity: Is synaptic plasticity an overly limited concept? *Progress in Brain Research, 138,* 91–108.

Huttenlocher, P. R. (1979). Synaptic density in human frontal cortex—developmental changes and effects of aging. *Brain Research, 163,* 195–205.

Maguire, E. A., Gadian, D. G., Johnsrude, I. S., Good, C. D., Ashburner, J., Frackowiak, R. S., & Frith, C. D. (2000). Navigation-related structural change in the hippocampi of taxi drivers. *Proceedings of the National Academy of Science, USA, 97*(8), 4398–4403.

Marks, H. M. (2000). Student engagement in instructional activity: Patterns in elementary, middle, and high school years. *American Educational Research Journal, 37,* 153–184.

McGivern, R. F., Andersen, J., Byrd, D., Mutter, K. L., & Reilly, J. (2002). Cognitive efficiency on a match to sample task decreases at the onset of puberty in children. *Brain and Cognition, 50,* 73–89.

Pashler, H. E. (1999). *The psychology of attention.* Boston: MIT Press.

Pintrich, P. (2004). A conceptual framework for assessing motivation and self-regulated learning in college students. *Educational Psychology Review, 16,* 385–407.

Powell, K. (2006). Neurodevelopment: How does the teenage brain work? *Nature, 442*(24), 865–867.

Reschly, A., Huebner, E., Appleton, J., & Antaramian, S. (2008). Engagement as flourishing: The contribution of positive emotions and coping to adolescents' engagement at school and with learning. *Psychology in the Schools, 45,* 419–431.

Rutter, M., & O'Connor, T. G. (2004). English and Romanian Adoptees (ERA) study team. Are there biological programming effects for psychological development? Findings from a study of Romanian adoptees. *Developmental Psychology, 40*(1), 81–94.

Sameroff, A. J. (1998). Environmental risk factors in infancy. *Pediatrics, 102*(5), 1287–1292.

Saudino, K. J. (2005). Behavioral genetics and child temperament. *Journal of Developmental and Behavioral Pediatrics, 26*(3), 214–223.

Schenk, J. (2011). *Teaching and the adolescent brain.* New York: W. W. Norton.

Schunk, D., & Zimmerman, B. (2003). Self-regulation and learning. In W. Reynolds & G. Miller (Eds.), *Handbook of Psychology: Vol. 7. Educational psychology* (pp. 59–78). New York: Wiley.

Skinner, E., Kinderman, T., & Furrer, C. (2009). A motivational perspective on engagement and disaffection: Conceptualization and assessment of children's behavioral and emotional participation in academic activities in the classroom. *Educational and Psychological Measurement, 69,* 493–525.

Skinner, E. A., Wellborn, J. G., & Connell, J. P. (1990). What it takes to do well in school and whether I've got it: The role of perceived control in children's engagement and school achievement. *Journal of Educational Psychology, 82,* 22–32.

Styles, E. A. (1997). *The psychology of attention.* London: Psychology Press.

Vrugt, A., & Oort, F. (2008). Metacognition, achievement goals, study strategies, and academic achievement: Pathways to achievement. *Metacognition and Learning, 3,* 123–146.

Wiesel, T. N., & Hubel, D. H. (1965). Extent of recovery from the effects of visual deprivation in kittens. *Journal of Neurophysiology, 28,* 1060–1072.

Wolfe, P. (2010). *Brain matters. Translating research into classroom practice* (2nd ed.). Alexandria, VA: Association for Supervision and Curriculum Development.

Yakovlev, P. A., & Lecours, I. R. (1967). The myelogenetic cycles of regional maturation of the brain. In A. Minkowski (Ed.), *Regional development of the brain in early life* (pp. 3–70). Oxford: Blackwell.

2

Building Background Knowledge

Background knowledge can be described as the essential information or key ingredients needed in order to understand the content
or learning. What students already know about the content—their
background knowledge—is one of the strongest predictors of how
well they will assimilate the new information related to that content
(Alexander, Kulikowich, & Jetton, 1994, 1995; Boulanger, 1981;
Duncan et al., 2007; Fennema, Franke, Carpenter, & Carey, 1993; La Paro
& Pianta, 2000; Pilburn, 1993; Pressley, Harris, & Marks, 1992;
Samson, Graue, Weinstein, & Walberg, 1984; Schneider, 1993; Schuler,
Funke, & Baron-Boldt, 1990; Spires & Donley, 1998; Tobias, 1994).
Enhancing a student's background knowledge should be a top con-
sideration when discussing methods of intervention used to raise
student achievement (Baniflower, Cohen, Pasley, & Weiss, 2008;
Bransford, Brown, & Cocking, 2000; Donovan & Bransford, 2005;
Hattie, 2009, 2012; Minstrell, 1989). Background knowledge is the
interaction of a student's ability to process and store information and
his or her academic experiences with that knowledge (Bransford et al.,
2000; Driver, Squires, Rushworth, & Wood-Robinson, 2005; Minstrell,
1989; National Research Council, 2007). Teachers will often suggest
that a lack of background knowledge contributes to their students'
lack of growth. Although a lack of background knowledge is often

seen as a barrier to student growth, we want to look past the barriers and conditions teachers feel they have no control over and concentrate on the techniques and strategies that we do have control over. If this background knowledge is not in place, we have to instill it ourselves. So what can you do to increase your students' background knowledge? Start with vocabulary!

This chapter actually has two goals: First, we seek to build your background knowledge regarding the parts of the brain, priming your brain for subsequent discussions. Second, we seek to model highly engaging techniques for building background knowledge, using particular vocabulary strategies. Background knowledge often manifests as vocabulary knowledge. Thus, the academic vocabulary of our science and math students is strongly associated with the breadth and depth of their background knowledge (Marzano, 2004; Marzano & Pickering, 2005). Recent research strongly suggests that the process of building academic background knowledge should include direct vocabulary instruction (Hattie, 2009, 2012; Marzano, 2004). Direct vocabulary instruction should (1) require students to develop descriptions of words, rather than just definitions; (2) incorporate both linguistic and nonlinguistic representations; (3) include multiple exposures to the words or concepts; (4) encourage students to discuss the words or concepts; (5) require students to play with words; and (6) focus on words that are necessary for academic success (Marzano, 2004; Marzano & Pickering, 2005). Now, let's apply these ideas as we build background knowledge on the parts of the brain.

Stop-n-Think Box 2.1

It would be quite a challenge to find an educator who has not heard something related to the brain and learning. What do you already know about the brain? What have you heard? Make a list of facts about the brain and learning.

Using Models to Build Background Knowledge

Believe it or not, the tools needed to introduce Neuroanatomy 101 are the same tools needed to hold this book: your two hands. Although the following demonstration may pose something of a challenge for you to do while reading at the same time, I assure you that the balancing act and effort are worth a try. First, clench each of your hands into a fist. Now press the two fists together at your first and second finger joints (see Figures 2.1 and 2.2).

Figure 2.1   Teachers Modeling a Brain

Figure 2.2   Students Modeling a Brain

Take a look. This is your brain! In fact, this is close to the actual size of the three-pound, highly efficient, and ever-so-important organ carefully mounted above your shoulders.

BRAIN FACTS

1. The average adult brain is 5.5 inches wide, 6.5 inches long, and 3.6 inches tall.

2. At birth, your brain weighed about 0.8 pounds. Now, it weighs about 3 pounds.

3. Your brain is approximately 78% water, 10% lipids, and 8% protein. (Smith, 2002; Society for Neuroscience, 2012a; Sylwester, 2005)

Now measure your "fist brain." Some of you reading this chapter may have expected a slightly larger brain and are now disappointed. For a different perspective, you may look at the fists of a colleague, knowing this is a fair estimate of the size of his or her brain, and think, "Now, that explains a lot." Just kidding! In any case, please relax your hands for the moment.

There are some incredibly interesting and shocking pieces of information about your brain that play an important role in keeping your science or math students activated, captivated, and invigorated. Let's tap into your background knowledge by challenging you with this True or False quiz. Following is a series of statements about the brain and learning. Some of the statements are true, others are false, and some are both true and false. The answers follow, and you may be surprised at which statements are actually myths.

1. You use 100% of your brain.

2. You stop growing new brain cells at the age of 18.

3. Boys and girls have different brains, and this translates into different academic behaviors.

4. Taking a break from studying to play video games actually helps students perform better on assignments.

5. Your brain uses about as much energy as a refrigerator light.

6. Language DVDs help your children learn to speak and read at a much faster rate.

7. Stress kills brain cells.

8. Learning is the brain's top priority.

9. Instant messaging and other social media are detrimental to the brain's ability to pay attention.

10. Playing Mozart for your students improves their performance in mathematics and reading.

Bonus: Emotions interfere with the type of learning that occurs in our classrooms.

1. T; 2. F; 3. F; 4. T; 5. T; 6. F; 7. T; 8. F; 9. Both; 10. F; Bonus: Both. (Jensen, 2005; Smith, 2002; Society for Neuroscience, 2012a, 2012b; Sylwester, 2005; Wolfe, 2010)

Were you surprised by the answers? Many of these statements are long-held beliefs about our brains and how our brains learn. The origins of neuromyths are often unknown, but they frequently show up in conversation and are agreed upon by everyone involved. For example, how many times have you heard that you only use 10% or 30% of your brain? This can depend on which "mythologist" was contributing to the conversation. The goal of this book is not to become the mythbusters of the brain world, but instead to use these intriguing statements to guide our discussion about keeping the student brain captivated, activated, and invigorated in science and mathematics classrooms. Look for these statements in the next several chapters. They will play an important role in linking each step of the recipe. However, to whet your appetite, let's look at a couple of these statements right now. How much of your brain do you really use?

Yes, you use 100% of your brain (Society for Neuroscience, 2012b). This is the good news.

BRAIN FACTS

1. Your brain accounts for 20% of the body's energy consumption.

2. The energy generated by your brain could light a 25-watt lightbulb.

3. More electrical impulses are generated in your brain per day than by all of the telephones in the world.

4. Scientists estimate that your brain generates approximately 70,000 thoughts per day. (Brain Health and Puzzles, 2012)

How efficiently you use 100% of your brain is a different issue altogether. As teachers, one of our many goals is to use teaching and learning strategies that improve upon and maximize the efficiency of the student brain. The next several chapters will share numerous strategies that help the brains of students in your science and mathematics classrooms work more efficiently and use a significant portion of the 70,000 thoughts believed to be generated by the human brain each day.

What is astonishing about the brain is that the energy needed to run our brains is approximately the same amount of energy needed to run a refrigerator lightbulb. Now that is efficient! What do we see when brains are not running efficiently? This situation might manifest as a learning disability, attention-deficit disorder, autism, or other challenging brain disorder. In each case, the brain is not running as efficiently as it should, and this affects learning and everyday life. On a less severe scale, classrooms that do not use the ingredients of the recipe introduced in Chapter 1 miss key opportunities for helping student brains work more efficiently. As a result, learning suffers.

A Road Map of the Brain

Stop-n-Think Box 2.2

Can you fill in the diagram of the brain in Figure 2.3? Use the word bank if you need it.

Figure 2.3   Diagram of the Brain

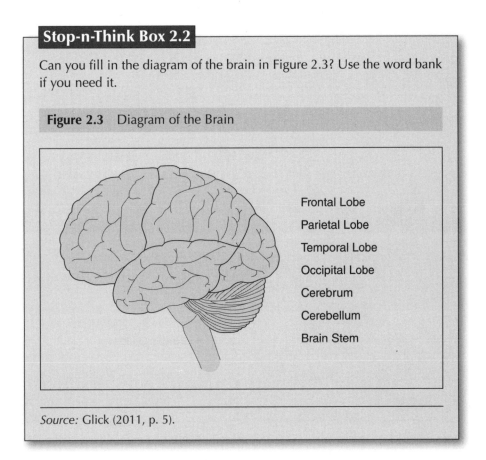

Frontal Lobe

Parietal Lobe

Temporal Lobe

Occipital Lobe

Cerebrum

Cerebellum

Brain Stem

Source: Glick (2011, p. 5).

Take another look at your "fist" model of the brain. The fact that our model requires a right and left fist, split down the middle, is perfect to illustrate the parts of our brains. Your brain does indeed have a right and left hemisphere. Although each hemisphere has its own list of favorites (e.g., the left hemisphere houses the language centers of the brain while the right hemisphere houses visual-spatial reasoning), the most efficient brains are constantly communicating between the two hemispheres by way of the corpus callosum (Jensen, 2005; Purves, Augustine, Fitzpatrick, Hall, & Lamantia, 2011; Reece et al., 2011; Society for Neuroscience, 2012a; Sylwester, 2005; Wolfe, 2010). The corpus callosum is collection of brain cells woven together to connect the right and left hemispheres (see Figure 2.4). Efficient brains happily communicate between the left and right hemispheres, integrating processes from both sides in order to engage in academic tasks like reading, writing, and mathematics problem solving. In the language of neuroscientists, efficient brains practice bihemispheric lateralization (Cheung, Chan, Chan, & Lam, 2006; Shevtsova & Reggia, 1999).

Figure 2.4 The Corpus Callosum

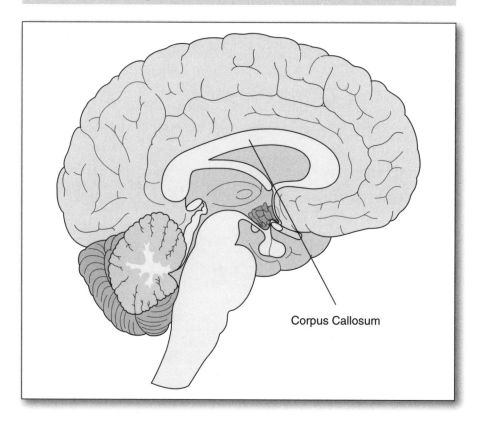

Corpus Callosum

In addition to the left and right hemispheres, the brain is composed of three major regions: the cerebrum, cerebellum, and brain stem (see Figure 2.5). Each of these regions has incredible responsibilities, not the least of which is learning. For example, the brain stem is responsible for the automatic processes of the body, such as breathing and keeping the heart beating. The cerebellum manages our gross motor movements as we run, skip, use a protractor, or participate in a hands-on science activity (Smith, 2002; Society for Neuroscience, 2012a; Sylwester, 2005). Much of the focus of this book will be on the cerebrum and the very interesting cerebral cortex.

Figure 2.5   The Three Major Regions and Four Lobes of the Brain

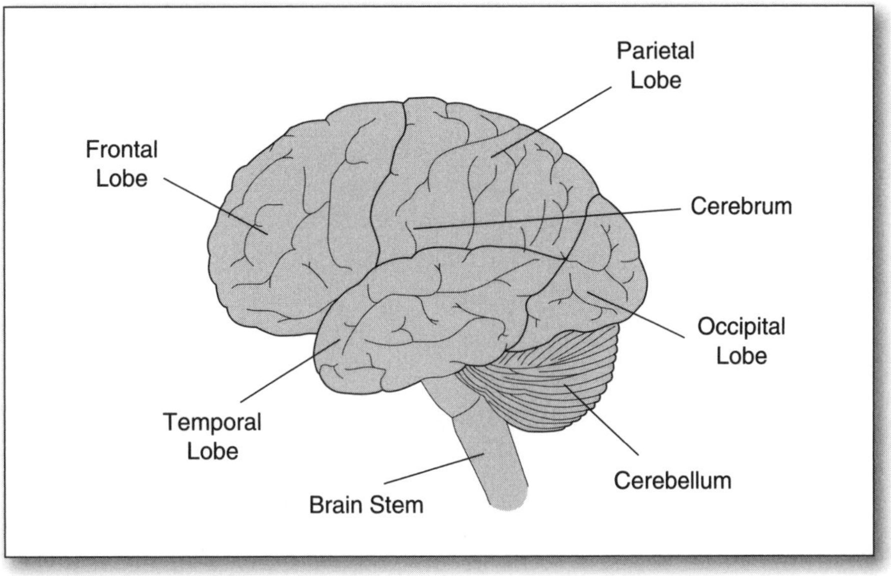

Source: Glick (2011, p. 5).

The cerebral cortex is a thin layer of brain cells wrapped around the entire cerebrum (Wolfe, 2010). This thin layer of brain cells is where much of the action occurs in which we, as teachers, are most interested. It contains peaks and valleys called *gyri* and *sulci*, respectively, that give it a lumpy appearance (Purves et al., 2011; Reece et al., 2011; Sylwester, 2005; Wolfe, 2010). The cerebral cortex plays a vital role in memory, attention, and thinking by forming connections, sparking networks of brain cells, and mixing together a collection of brain chemicals.

BRAIN FACTS

Why is the brain "lumpy"? Well, it actually has to do with math, in particular geometry and surface area. The cerebral cortex makes up about 85% of the brain. To maximize the surface area and still keep all of the real estate associated with the cerebral cortex, evolution decided to wrinkle it up (Smith, 2002; Sylwester, 2005).

The cerebral cortex is subdivided into the frontal, temporal, parietal, and occipital cortices or lobes. These sensory, motor, and association areas process visual, auditory, and tactile input; plan the execution of our most finely tuned movements; and blend together our experiences for storage in long-term memory (Reece et al., 2011). Table 2.1 summarizes the key areas of the cerebral cortex and the role these areas may play in learning.

Table 2.1   The Brain's Lobes

Lobes of the Cerebral Cortex	Function and Role in Learning	Where Is the lobe?
Occipital Lobe	Primary region for processing visual stimuli; responsible for perceiving visual information and then checking to see whether the visual stimuli are familiar (i.e., "that is a trapezoid" or "that is an angiosperm").	Occipital Lobe
Temporal Lobe	Primary region for processing auditory stimuli; includes areas responsible for hearing, language, and memory; like the occipital lobe, the temporal lobe is responsible for perceiving auditory information and then checking to see if we recognize what we are hearing.	Temporal Lobe

Lobes of the Cerebral Cortex	Function and Role in Learning	Where Is the lobe?
Parietal Lobe	Primary region for processing spatial awareness and orientation; responsible for receiving sensory stimuli such as touch, temperature, and pain; also helps the brain know where each part of the body is located relative to the surroundings; helps maintain spatial attention.	Parietal Lobe
Frontal Lobe	Processes the most complex human functions including executive functions (e.g., thinking about consequences, making decisions about good versus bad actions, suppressing unacceptable social options, mediating emotional responses, identifying similarities and differences, and retaining long-term memories for non-task-based activities.	Frontal Lobe

Sources: Adapted from Wolfe (2010). Images adapted from Glick (2011, p. 5).

Stop-n-Think Box 2.3

Take a second and review the brain terminology presented thus far in the chapter. Summarize to yourself or share your brain information with a colleague. Review these terms about the brain:

1. Bihemispheric lateralization
2. Corpus callosum
3. Cerebral cortex
4. Cerebellum
5. Brain stem
6. Cerebrum

The Nuts and Bolts

What makes up a brain? For the biology teachers reading this book, this might be a "gimme." For those of us who teach physics or geometry, this is a fair question. The answer: brain cells. There are two main types of brain cells: those involved in thinking (neurons) and those supporting the brain cells doing the thinking (glia; Wolfe, 2010). Although glia are extremely important and valuable, we focus our discussion on the neurons and how to put them to use. These microscopic cells form connections and networks that represent the knowledge and understanding our students take away from our science and mathematics classes. Instead of "there's an app for that," when students successfully recall the trends on the periodic table, the solution to a rational equation, the parts of the rock cycle, or the correct conversion from logarithmic form to exponential form, there is a network for that! In fact, if the network is not there, the knowledge is not there either (Hebb, 1949; Jensen, 2005).

Much like your two-fisted representation of the brain, the best model of a neuron is found on your body. Please hold up either hand and take a look at your hand and arm. This is a model of a neuron, starting at your fingertips, right down to the elbow, or olecranon (the scientific term for the elbow). If you wiggle your fingers, you are also wiggling super-enlarged dendrites. The palm of your hand represents the cell body, and your arm represents the axon (see Figure 2.6).

Figure 2.6   Making Neurons

Stop-n-Think Box 2.4

Can you fill in the diagram of the neuron in Figure 2.7?

Figure 2.7   Diagram of the Neuron

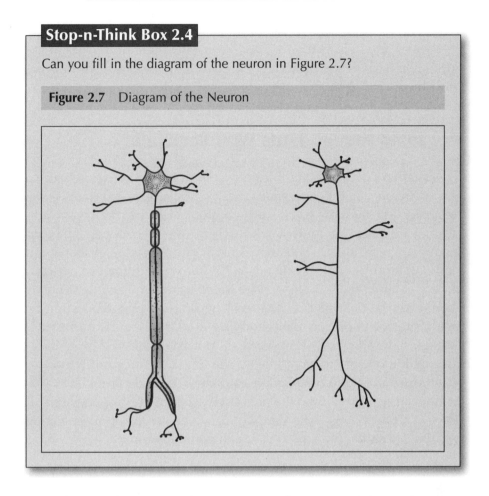

When we learn something new or take in new information, our brain stores this new knowledge as a connection between neurons. The dendrite of one neuron gets very, very close to the axon of other neurons. These two brain cells do not actually touch, but maintain a small distance between them called the *synapse*.

When brain cells communicate, an electrical signal is sent down the axon, which activates the release of chemicals known as *neurotransmitters*. Neurotransmitters swim across the synapse and activate the connecting neuron. They trigger another electrical signal that travels down the second neuron. This process, chemical-electrical-chemical, is the main method of communication for our brains and our students' brains (Purves et al., 2011; Smith, 2002; Sylwester, 2005; Wolfe, 2010).

Those are the brain basics! This overview of your brain and brain cells provides the background knowledge for the rest of the book. Chapters 3 through 7 revisit these major structures and add new ones that are relevant to the discussion. For example, there is a collection of brain cells in the brain stem that respond quite nicely to novelty and help students filter out irrelevant stimuli (flies in the room, the hum of the projector, etc.) and let in relevant stimuli (the stuff they need to learn).

Engaging the Students With Vocabulary

This chapter contains a significant amount of terminology related to the brain. As science and mathematics teachers, we recognize the necessity for students to be very comfortable with the vocabulary needed to learn the content we teach in our classrooms. Take, for example, the difference between "speed" and "velocity." What about "cations" and "anions" in chemistry? What is the difference between an equilateral, an isosceles, and a right triangle? Having students memorize the definition of the term by first copying the definition into their notebook and then studying it ad nauseam is not exactly engaging. In addition, if students do not have the necessary background knowledge to comprehend the text, they may not know, for example, that they have seen an equilateral triangle in real life. Not only will the "copy down the definition" strategy not be engaging; it also won't work! So what can we do? Let's see what an engaging vocabulary strategy might look like in your classroom.

Wage a Bet

- Divide your class into small groups, about four student per group.
- Give each group a 3 × 3 table already printed, or have them drawn one on a sheet of paper.

- Select nine essential concepts, terms, or learnings associated with the unit the class is currently working on or has recently completed.
- After posting these terms either on poster paper, whiteboard, or SMART Board, have the students randomly write one term in each box.

- Now tell the groups to assign each term one of the following values, based on their collective knowledge of that content: 100, 150, 200, 250, 300, 350, 400, 450, 500.
- The goal is to obtain the highest number of points. The teacher either gives a problem or asks a question in each area. After each question, the groups put their heads together to come up with an answer or solution.
- If the group gives the correct response, they circle the point value. If the group does not get it right, they cross out the point value. After all the nine questions are asked, the students add up their points.

Here is a Math example:

Direct the student groups to write one term in each box of their 3 × 3 table. (Location does not matter.)

1. Vertical angles

2. Consecutive interior angles

3. Corresponding angles

4. Complimentary angles

5. Alternate exterior angles

6. Linear pair

7. Supplementary angles

8. Alternate interior angles

9. Adjacent angles

Ask the groups to assign one of the following values to each term and write that value in the corresponding box: 100, 150, 200, 250, 300, 350, 400, 450, 500.

Remind students that the values indicate how confident their group is that it will answer a question about that term correctly. For example, a group's table may look like Table 2.2.

Next, present Figure 2.8.

Ask the following questions orally, or put them on a PowerPoint, or SMART Board.

Vertical angles

Q: If ∠3 is vertical with ∠2, and ∠3 is 60°, what do we know about angles 1 and 4?

A: They are vertical angles as well.

Table 2.2 Math Terms

Corresponding angles 300	Adjacent angles 100	Supplementary angles 500
Alternate exterior angles 350	Vertical angles 250	Linear pair 200
Consecutive interior angles 50	Complimentary angles 450	Alternate interior angles 150

Figure 2.8 Parallel Lines Cut by a Transversal

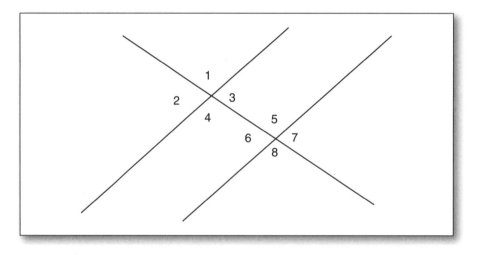

Consecutive interior angles

Q: Are consecutive interior angles supplementary? Give two examples.

A: Yes, they are supplementary. Examples: ∠4 and ∠6, and ∠3 and ∠5.

Corresponding angles

Q: Where do we find corresponding angles? Provide two examples in Figure 2.8.

A: On parallel lines, these two angles are on the same side of the transverse and the same side of the parallel lines.

Any of these pairs: ∠2 and ∠6, ∠4 and ∠8, ∠1 and ∠5, or ∠3 and ∠7.

Complimentary angles

    Q: Using Figure 2.8, explain where you find a pair of complimentary angles.

    A: There aren't any (two angles that add up to 90°).

Alternate exterior angles

    Q: Are alternate exterior angles congruent? Give an example.

    A: Yes they are congruent; examples are $\angle 2$ and $\angle 7$ or $\angle 1$ and $\angle 8$.

Linear pair

    Q: If $\angle 6$ is 60°, which angle would form a linear pair with $\angle 6$? And what would be the measurement of that angle?

    A: Angle 5, and it would be 120°, or $\angle 8$ and it would be 120°.

Supplementary angles

    Q: What is the maximum number of supplementary angles you can find?

    A: 12. $\angle 1$ and $\angle 2$, $\angle 3$ and $\angle 4$, $\angle 1$ and $\angle 3$, $\angle 2$ and $\angle 4$, $\angle 5$ and $\angle 7$, $\angle 7$ and $\angle 8$, $\angle 8$ and $\angle 6$, $\angle 6$ and $\angle 5$, $\angle 3$ and $\angle 5$, $\angle 4$ and $\angle 6$, $\angle 2$ and $\angle 8$, and $\angle 1$ and $\angle 7$.

Alternate interior angles

    Q: Explain the difference between an alternate exterior angle and an alternate interior angle. Give an example of an alternate interior angle.

    A: They are on opposite sides of the transversal; however, the alternate exterior angles are on the outside of the transversal, and the alternate interior angles are on the inside of the transversal. For example, $\angle 4$ and $\angle 5$ or $\angle 3$ and $\angle 6$.

Adjacent angles

    Q: Are $\angle 3$ and $\angle 5$ adjacent angles ? Why or why not? Provide a definition of adjacent angles.

    A: Angle 3 and $\angle 5$ are not adjacent because they do not have a common vertex and side. Adjacent angles are two angles that share a common vertex and side but have no common interior points.

After each question, give students enough time to come up with their answers. Engage them in a discussion that extends their thought process. We want a good "math talk" session, so other students understand the rationale for their answer.

Beach Ball Vocabulary

1. Get some cheap beach balls and water-based, overhead projector markers.

2. Put students into small groups of three or four students.

3. Ask each group to select a key concept or term that is necessary for success in your science or mathematics classroom.

4. Instruct each group to fill the panels of their beach ball with words or phrases, pictures, and examples or nonexamples— without using the concept or term.

5. Have the students form a circle in the room and toss the beach balls like a hot potato.

6. When "time" is called, each individual holding a ball picks one panel and determines what concept or term is represented by that particular panel.

7. The beach ball panels can also be deciphered as a small group activity.

Beach Ball Vocabulary has a number of learning benefits. The students are collaboratively developing multiple linguistic and nonlinguistic representations, which will result in a high degree of understanding for all students. The teacher could also increase student accountability by giving each group member a different color marker and expect each member to contribute to the information on the beach ball. As the game continues, students quickly become aware that they may eventually be the one responsible for sharing with the group their thoughts about the concept or vocabulary term represented on their ball. This also increases on-task behavior and increases accountability for learning. This strategy could be used as a method for developing a deeper understanding of concepts about to be learned, or it could be an effective closure activity to review concepts and terms previously learned; in addition, students will have fun tossing the balls around the room. It is important that students understand the concepts and terms in their unit of study. Beach Ball Vocabulary offers that learning focus.

Word Wall

Is it really okay to play in science and math class? The answer to this question is yes. One of the many ways to encourage students to play with concepts, terms, and vocabulary is with a Word Wall. Attach a large sheet of paper to one wall of your classroom and designate that area as the Word Wall for a particular unit or topic. There are a couple of variations on this strategy with respect to the amount of teacher involvement. One approach is for you, the teacher, to scatter the concepts, terms, or vocabulary all over the Word Wall. A second option would be to have students participate in a prereading or brainstorming activity in which the students generate a list of concepts, terms, or vocabulary for the wall.

Teacher: *Good morning! To start class today, you will need your textbook, a sheet of paper, and something to write with.*

Teacher pauses and waits for students to gather materials.

Teacher: *Great. Please check with your neighbors and make sure they have their textbook, a sheet of paper, and something to write with. If they do, give me a thumbs-up. If not, please help them out.*

Teacher pauses and waits for students to give the thumbs-up signal.

Teacher: *Please find page 105 in your textbooks, the first page of the chapter on plant structure and growth. When you are there, give me a thumbs-up.*

Teacher pauses and waits for students to give the thumbs-up signal.

Teacher: *Please look through the chapter and make a list of 10 to 15 concepts, terms, or words that you think are important in the chapter. See if you can get 10 to 15 on your list in two minutes. GO!*

Regardless of whether you use a teacher-generated list or a student-generated list, these words should be scattered on the Word Wall for students to see and use in context every day. For example, you might have students pick two or three words and explain their meaning to a neighbor. Students might be asked to select one or two words and create a visual sketch of the terms. As an exit activity, students might pick the concepts, terms, or vocabulary from the day's lesson and create a few sentences that conceptually link the words together. The key is to have your students interact with each other and the words on a regular basis.

Stop-n-Think Box 2.5

Generate your own ideas for using a Word Wall.

Write It, Draw It, Apply It

To ensure multiple exposures and representations of the concepts, terms, and vocabulary necessary for academic success, have students create a chart on which they write a definition of the word (Write It), draw a visual representation of the word (Draw It), and then provide a concrete example (Apply It; see Table 2.4).

Table 2.4   Vocabulary Worksheet

Concept, Term, or Vocabulary	Write It (Definition)	Draw It (Visual)	Apply It (Example)
Parallel lines	Two or more coplanar lines that have no points in common.	_____ _____	
Centrifugal force	A force that keeps a body moving with a uniform speed along a circular path and is directed along the radius toward the center.		

Now it is your turn. Please select a specific unit or concept that is part of your curriculum. For example, you may decide to use quadratic equations, linear momentum, geologic processes, or acid-base theory. Create a list of concepts, terms, and vocabulary that are necessary for academic success in this unit or concept.

Concepts, Terms, and Vocabulary

Now that you have your list of concepts, terms, and vocabulary, how will you help students develop a conceptual understanding of the list? Use Table 2.3 to reflect and develop your own ideas.

Table 2.3 Direct Vocabulary

Characteristics of direct vocabulary instruction	Examples modeled in this chapter	How would you use it with your list?
Descriptions, not definitions		
Linguistic and nonlinguistic		
Multiple exposures		
Student discussion		
Play		

Pandora's Box

The phrase "opening Pandora's box" implies that someone is about to unleash something that is both negative and irreversible. During parent conferences, if a teacher decided to inform a parent that his or her child would never get into Harvard, that teacher would certainly be opening Pandora's box. However, the astute Greek mythology student would know that this is not the whole story. In fact, when Pandora opened the box that contained all of the evils of the world, not everything escaped. What was left in the box? Hope. Each student who occupies a desk in your science or mathematics classroom possesses a three-pound, fully functional brain that should be our source of hope. Amid all of the challenges we face in the classroom, it is our belief that an understanding of how this brain works and what type of environment best maximizes the efficiency of this brain is, indeed, a source of hope. Hope for engaging each of our students in science and mathematics and helping them build the necessary background knowledge to be successful. Starting with a basic understanding of the brain, we are in a much better position to tackle questions like, Why did my students forget what we did yesterday? How can I help students make meaningful connections? Are there ways to enhance how my students will acquire background knowledge? and Can I really help my students' brains work more efficiently? We are just beginning to answer these questions.

CHAPTER 2: CONCEPT DEVELOPMENT EXIT TICKET

The exit ticket below is a model for assessing student understanding of key concepts and vocabulary. For the purposes of modeling, complete the exit ticket below using the concept *background knowledge*. On a scale of 1 to 4, with 4 being the highest, how would you rate your understanding of the importance of background knowledge? In your own words, write a summary of the importance of background knowledge. Finally, develop a visual representation of the term *background knowledge,* and list examples for generating and developing background knowledge.

Photo from Thinkstock.com.

Concept: Background Knowledge   **My Understanding: 1 2 3 4**

Summary: _____

_____

_____

Drawing   **More Ideas**

The preceding exit ticket could be used for any concept in science or mathematics. For example, instead of background knowledge, you could use the rock cycle, the Pythagorean theorem, rational functions, atmospheric pressure, and so on.

Engaging Professional Development Tasks

1. This professional development task incorporates strategies utilized by your colleagues to assess and build background knowledge. Ask several colleagues to share their thoughts on the background knowledge of their students. How do they assess the background knowledge of their students? How do they incorporate these findings into their teaching? How do they address the issue of low background knowledge or misconceptions? What about students who have a high level of background knowledge? Collect several ideas that are different from your own and try them out in your classroom.

2. This professional development task helps you develop strategies for teaching essential concepts, terms, and vocabulary in your classroom. Create a list of essential concepts, terms, and vocabulary for a specific unit of study. Another option is to use the list developed earlier in this chapter and create a series of specific, ready-to-use strategies that span the unit of study. Develop a timeline for implementation based on when these strategies would be most effective within the unit plan. Consider these questions in your planning:

   - How would you cluster concepts, terms, and vocabulary together for the unit?
   - What concepts, terms, and vocabulary are necessary to start the unit?
   - What terminology can be introduced later in the unit because it builds on earlier terminology?

References

Alexander, P. A., Kulikowich, J. M., & Jetton, T. L. (1994). The role of subject-matter knowledge and interest in the processing of linear and nonlinear texts. *Review of Educational Research, 64,* 201–252.

Alexander, P. A., Kulikowich, J. M., & Jetton, T. L. (1995). Interrelationship of knowledge, interest, and recall: Assessing a model of domain learning. *Journal of Educational Psychology, 87*(4), 559–575.

Baniflower, E., Cohen, K., Pasley, J., & Weiss, I. (2008). *Effective science instruction: What does research tell us?* Portsmouth, NH: RMC Research Corporation, Center on Instruction.

Boulanger, F. D. (1981). Instruction and science learning: A quantitative synthesis. *Journal of Research in Science Teaching, 18*(4), 311–327.

Brain Health and Puzzles. (2012). *Fun facts about the brain.* Retrieved January 15, 2012, from http://www.brainhealthandpuzzles.com/fun_facts_about_the_brain.html

Bransford, J., Brown, A., & Cocking, R. (Eds.). (2000). *How people learn: Brain, mind, experience, and school: Expanded edition.* Washington, DC: National Academies Press.

Cheung, M., Chan, A. S., Chan, Y., & Lam, J. M. K. (2006). Language lateralization of Chinese-English bilingual patients with temporal lobe epilepsy: A functional MRI study. *Neuropsychology, 20*(5), 589–597.

Donovan, S., & Bransford, J. (Eds.). (2005). *How students learn: Science in the classroom.* Washington, DC: National Academies Press.

Driver, R., Squires, A., Rushworth, P., & Wood-Robinson, V. (2005). *Making sense of secondary science: Research into children's ideas.* New York: Routledge.

Duncan, G. J., Dowsett, C. J., Claessens, A., Magnuson, K., Huston, A. C., Klebanov, P., . . . Japel, C. (2007). School readiness and later achievement. *Developmental Psychology, 43*(6), 1428–1446.

Fennema, E., Franke, M. L., Carpenter, T. P., & Carey, D. A. (1993). Using children's mathematical knowledge in instruction. *American Educational Research Journal, 30*(3), 555–583.

Glick, M. (2011). *The instructional leader and the brain: Using neuroscience to inform practice.* Thousand Oaks, CA: Corwin.

Hattie, J. A. C. (2009). *Visible learning. A synthesis of over 800 meta-analyses relating to achievement.* New York: Routledge.

Hattie, J. A. C. (2012). *Visible learning for teachers. Maximizing impact on learning.* New York: Routledge.

Hebb, D. O. (1949). *The organization of behavior.* New York: Wiley & Sons.

Jensen, E. (2005). *Teaching with the brain in mind* (2nd ed.). Alexandria, VA: Association for Supervision and Curriculum Development.

La Paro, K. M., & Pianta, R. C. (2000). Predicting children's competence in the early school years: A meta-analytic review. *Review of Educational Research, 70*(4), 443–484.

Marzano, R. J. (2004). *Building background knowledge for academic achievement. Research on what works in schools.* Alexandria, VA: Association for Supervision and Curriculum Development.

Marzano, R. J., & Pickering, D. J. (2005). *Building academic vocabulary: Teacher's manual.* Alexandria, VA: Association for Supervision and Curriculum Development.

Minstrell, J. (1989). Teaching science for understanding. In L. B. Resnick & L. E. Klopfer (Eds.), *Toward the thinking curriculum: Current cognitive research* (pp. 129–149). Alexandria, VA: Association for Supervision and Curriculum Development.

National Research Council. (2007). *Taking science to school: Learning and teaching science in grades K–8.* Washington, DC: The National Academies Press.

Pilburn, M. D. (1993, April). *Evidence from meta-analysis for an expert model of achievement in science.* Paper presented at the Annual Meeting of the National Association for Research in Science Teaching, Atlanta, GA.

Pressley, M., Harris, K. R., & Marks, M. B. (1992). But good strategy instructors are constructivists! *Educational Psychology Review, 4,* 3–31.

Purves, D., Augustine, G. J., Fitzpatrick, D., Hall, W. C., & Lamantia, A. S. (Eds.). (2011). *Neuroscience* (5th ed.). Sunderland, MA: Sinauer Associates.

Reece, J. B., Urry, M. L., Cain, M. L., Wasserman, S. A., Minorsky, P. V., & Jackson, R. B. (2011). *Campbell biology* (9th ed.). San Francisco: Pearson Education.

Samson, G. E., Graue, M. E., Weinstein, T., & Walberg, H. J. (1984). Academic and occupational performance: A quantitative synthesis. *American Educational Research Journal, 21*(2), 311–321.

Schneider, W. (1993). Domain-specific knowledge and memory performance in children. *Educational Psychology Review, 5*, 257–273.

Schuler, H., Funke, U., & Baron-Boldt, J. (1990). Predictive validity of school grades: A meta-analysis. *Applied Psychology: An International Review, 39*(1), 89–103.

Shevtsova, N., & Reggia, J. (1999). Lateralization in a bihemispheric neural model of letter identification. *Neurocomputing, 26*, 875–880.

Smith, A. (2002). *The brain's behind it: New knowledge about the brain and learning.* Stafford, UK: Network Educational Press.

Society for Neuroscience. (2012a). *Brain facts. A primer on the brain and nervous system.* Washington, DC: Author.

Society for Neuroscience. (2012b). *Neuromyths.* Retrieved January 15, 2012, from http://www.brainfacts.org/neuromyths/

Spires, H. A., & Donley, J. (1998). Prior knowledge activation: Inducing engagement with informational texts. *Journal of Educational Psychology, 90*(2), 249–260.

Sylwester, R. (2005). *How to explain a brain. An educator's handbook of brain terms and cognitive processes.* Thousand Oaks, CA: Corwin.

Tobias, S. (1994). Interest, prior knowledge, and learning. *Review of Educational Research, 63*, 37–54.

Wolfe, P. (2010). *Brain matters: Translating research into classroom practice.* (2nd ed.). Alexandria, VA: Association for Supervision and Curriculum Development.

3

Prime the Brain

Activate Prior Knowledge

The Deafening Sound of Silence

As the tardy bell rings and the halls finally clear, we often start class with what we believe is a very simple and straightforward question: Who can tell me what we did yesterday? What follows is an awkward and often aggravating silence. However, brain researchers would argue that this is a predictable and normal response that can be avoided. Jump-starting the student brain and activating prior knowledge is a daily, necessary, and important task in our science and math classrooms. In fact, every day, each lesson or learning segment should begin with an exercise that requires students to tap into their prior knowledge about a particular topic. The background knowledge of our students lacks the breadth and depth of our own background knowledge, and thus, explicit strategies must be used to facilitate the activation of this knowledge. Yet, time restraints and the volume of content that is expected to be covered in a middle school or high school science or mathematics class force us to forgo this extremely important part of student learning. As highlighted in the previous chapter, research strongly suggests that prior knowledge is one of the most significant factors contributing to individual differences in the classroom. So let's start with two questions. One, would you be interested in a few strategies that would enable your students to encode, retain, and recall information more successfully? And two, would you like to reduce the amount of time you spend reteaching content? If you answered yes to both of these questions, then setting aside time each day for your students to activate prior knowledge should be on the top of your strategy list. Beginning each day, lesson, or learning segment with exercises that enable students to recall what they already know about a topic provides two brain benefits: (1) it enables the brain to work more efficiently, and (2) it enables students to encode, retain, and recall information more successfully (Raichle et al., 1994; Schacter & Buckner, 1998; Schacter, Dobbins, & Schnyer, 2004; Schacter, Wig, & Stevens, 2007; Squire et al., 1992; Wig, Buckner, & Schacter, 2009).

Stop-n-Think Box 3.2

Glance back at the strategies, activities, and questions you listed in Stop-n-Think Box 3.1. Which of these strategies activate the prior knowledge of your students? Spend a few minutes thinking about how you could modify your approach so that students will be tapping into their prior knowledge.

Making Student Brains More Efficient

Simply put, brains work more efficiently when new learning is linked to prior learning. The student brain is better able to integrate new learning if there is a conceptual framework already in place (Mayer, 1989). In other words, if the brain already has a framework for incorporating the new learning, it does not have to both create a conceptual framework and learn the new material. When teachers provide an opportunity for students to activate prior knowledge, they increase the probability that the students will personally relate to the new learning and thus engage more efficiently in meaningful learning and elaboration. If students have not accessed prior knowledge, they often rely on rote learning and memorization because they lack the capacity to make meaning of the new learning (Ormrod, 2011).

Another way to look at this increase in efficiency is to look at the brain in terms of available resources or "brain food." The brain requires energy to function and gets this energy from glucose via the blood-brain barrier and oxygen (Sylwester, 2005). Similarly, the brain's processing capacity is dependent upon our working memory system (see, e.g., classic studies like Miller, 1956, and Peterson & Peterson, 1959) and brain structures like the hippocampus (Laroche, Davis, & Jay, 2000; Manns, Hopkins, & Squire, 2003; Squire, 1992). Neuroscience research that looks at the levels of activation in regions of the brain responsible for learning and memory enables scientists to study how these levels vary when prior knowledge exists (e.g., Buckner et al., 1995; Buckner, Koutstaal, Schacter, & Rosen, 2000; Squire et al., 1992; Tulving & Schacter, 1990; Wagner, Desmond, Demb, Glover, & Gabrieli, 1997). These studies suggest that if the student has the necessary prior knowledge at his or her fingertips—or, as you may recall from the previous chapter, dendrites—less brain activation, and thus fewer resources, are needed to engage the student in meaningful learning. These resources are then available for other cognitive, behavioral, and emotional tasks. On the other hand, if a student has not activated prior knowledge, a larger proportion of the brain's resources are used for processing and learning the new knowledge and is therefore not available for other cognitive, behavioral, and emotional tasks.

Getting Better Encoding, Retention, and Recall

If the brain is working more efficiently when prior knowledge is activated, does it also mean that students are more successfully encoding, retaining, and recalling the information? The answer is yes. The activation of prior knowledge and the association with better encoding, retention, and recall has been well studied for decades (e.g., Alexander, Kulikowich, & Schulze, 1994; DeWitt, Knight, Hicks, & Ball, 2012; Schneider, 1993; Tobias, 1994). In almost all of these studies, prior knowledge about a particular topic or content area increased the ability of the study participants to encode, retain, and recall new information about that particular topic or content area. Whether it is a lesson on atmospheric pressure, trends in the periodic table, photosynthesis, or simple machines, how much students ultimately learn in our science and mathematics classes is strongly associated with how much they already know about the topic.

So how do we facilitate this activation of prior knowledge in our classrooms? The rule of thumb for this strategy is "more of them, less of you." In other words, strategies for activating prior knowledge should require them to dig out the information and not involve us telling them "what we did yesterday, last week, or last year."

Stop-n-Think Box 3.3

Revisit your list of prior knowledge strategies in Stop-n-Think Box 3.2. How many of these strategies are teacher directed versus student centered? How could you tweak the strategy to encourage more involvement by the student?

Now let's look at several examples of strategies that activate prior knowledge; help brains work more efficiently; promote better encoding, retention, and recall; and follow the rule of thumb, "more of them, less of you." Many of the examples presented in this chapter and throughout the book contain vignettes to suggest how they might best be implemented in the classroom. The vignettes provide very precise language that may appear unnecessary. However, the language is extremely important for the engagement of our students' brains. Science and mathematics teachers often overlook these very subtle instructions because we possess a strong foundational knowledge base that enables us to have a clear picture of the outcome of a task and the path that leads to reaching that outcome. This is an example of our expertise working against us. We have to stair-step, scaffold, and ease our students through the complexities of our content.

Brainstorming

Teacher: *Good afternoon! To start class today, you will need your notes from yesterday's class, your textbook, a sheet of paper, and something to write with.*

Teacher pauses and waits for students to gather materials.

Teacher: *Great. Please check with your neighbors and make sure they have their notes from yesterday, their textbook, a sheet of paper, and something to write with. If they do, tell them, "Nice job." If not, please help them out.*

Teacher pauses and waits for students to check with their neighbors.

Teacher: *Yesterday we talked about the algebraic properties. Please find that section of your textbook. Look up once you have found that section.*

Teacher pauses and waits for students to make eye contact.

Teacher: *Using your notes from yesterday and your textbook, create a random word splash or develop a list of important words, phrases, or examples from those two sources. Let's see how many you can list in three minutes. GO!*

Brainstorming is a familiar strategy that can be used to encourage students to revisit previous material and identify words, phrases, or concepts that they believe to be important and have meaning. This strategy can be done individually, with a partner, or as a group activity. For example, a teacher could arrange students into groups of three or four and provide them with a big idea or concept from a previous lesson that would be considered prior knowledge for the topic of the day. Student groups would generate their brainstorming lists much like the vignette, but as a cooperative learning task.

After the group has developed a list of ideas on a large sheet of poster paper, the activity continues.

Teacher: *Please pause where you are and put the cap on your marker. Now that each group has a brainstorming list on their poster paper, let's compare them. Please find a place on the wall to hang up your brainstorming poster.*

Teacher pauses and waits for student groups to hang up their poster paper.

Teacher: *As a group, you will be given the opportunity to rotate from poster to poster to check out and discuss other groups' lists. If you believe another group's poster needs a word, phrase, or additional example, please add it using your group's unique colored marker. That way, we know which group added information. You have two minutes at each poster. I will initiate the transitions by playing music. So each time you hear the music begin, please rotate to the poster on your right. GO!*

As a debriefing activity, ask students to justify what they added to the poster. This is also an excellent time for you to clear up any misconceptions, offer additional information, and add your own words as well.

There are many ways to engage your class in brainstorming activities. Have you ever tried to engage your entire class in a brainstorming session, only to find that one or two students quickly offered many ideas within the first few seconds, while others were distracted because they needed a few minutes of processing time to think? Centerpiece is a brainstorming strategy that allows for flexibility in thinking time. Students sit in a group, and each student is given a piece of paper. There is also an extra sheet of paper in the middle of the table. When the teacher announces the topic, each student is expected to write one response on the sheet of paper in front of him or her and then exchange that sheet paper with the one in the middle of the table. Consequently, the sheet in the middle of the table rotates continually. This allows students who have lots of ideas to get those ideas on paper quickly, while the other students have time to process their thoughts. At the end of the time given, the papers are arranged end to end, providing a list of ideas from the whole group. The group can then be given the option to cross off duplications or combine items for a more comprehensive response. Centerpiece is really a way to differentiate processing time for your students. There are many ways to add structure to a brainstorming session. By doing so, teachers will not only ensure individual accountability, but equal participation, simultaneous interaction, and positive interdependence among the students.

David Sousa (2011) believes that this revisiting of past learning provides a great opportunity for students to transfer knowledge to present learning. Other brain researchers agree with this idea. Willingham and Daniel (2012) assert that one of the most effective ways to remember something is to recall it. Furthermore, the brainstorming of words, phrases, or concepts promotes the identification of critical attributes of the topic and the association of those words, phrases, or concepts with a particular big idea (Sousa, 2011). So what else can we do with the brainstorming list? Content that is organized in a meaningful way is much easier to learn and remember than is a simple list of words (Anderson, 1983; Durso & Coggins, 1991).

Concept Maps, Knowledge Maps, and Mind Maps

One way to help students organize information in a meaningful way is to ask them to create a mind map. Also referred to as a "concept map" or "knowledge map," these graphic organizers are visual representations of knowledge that use connecting lines and figures to show relationships among concepts, processes, or other ideas

(Alvermann, 1981; Ives & Hoy, 2003; Nesbit & Adesope, 2006; Winn, 1991). Believe it or not, the invention of the concept map is attributed to David Ausubel (1968) and was part of his theory on meaningful learning. Ausubel believed that learners actively subsume new concepts within a conceptual framework or structure of prior knowledge (Estes, Mills, & Barron, 1969). That is, a concept map enables students to take new concepts and actively organize them into a visual representation of their cognitive understanding of existing knowledge.

Research on the instructional benefits of concept maps in instructional settings is quite positive. The use of concept maps is associated with an increase in encoding, retention, and recall (Nesbit & Adesope, 2006). From a meta-analysis of more than 500 peer-reviewed studies, researchers identified a variety of uses for concept maps, including individually and cooperatively generated maps from lectures or printed materials, maps as advance organizers, collaboration tools, and stand-alone collections of information (Novak & Gowin, 1984; see also O'Donnell, Dansereau, & Hall, 2002). Studies indicate that when concept maps are used in conjunction with text or lectures, used to convert text into a visual representation, or used in cooperative learning tasks and peer teaching, students demonstrate a higher level of understanding and retention of knowledge (Foos, 1995; Griffin & Robinson, 2005; see also Holliday, Brunner, & Donais, 1977; Horton et al., 1993; Patterson, Dansereau, & Wiegmann, 1993). In addition, low-ability, low-background students demonstrate a greater benefit than their high-ability, high-background classmates, making the use of concepts maps vital for meeting the needs of all learners (Stensvold & Wilson, 1990).

Here is another way to utilize the posters developed by the students.

Teacher: *As you return to your seats, please get out a clean sheet of paper.*

Teacher pauses and waits for students to return to their seats and get out a sheet of paper.

Teacher: *On your sheet of paper, draw a circle in the center of your paper that is about the size of an egg yolk. You will be using a variety of the colored markers at your table to arrange the words, phrases, or examples from your posters hanging on the wall into a mind map.*

Teacher shows an example of a mind map (Figure 3.1).

Figure 3.1   Mind Map

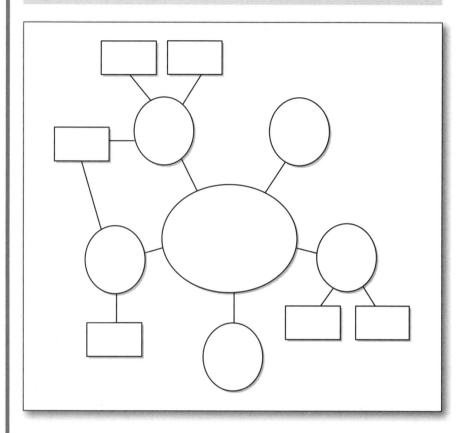

Teacher: *Here is an example of a mind map. Notice how I have used col-*
ored lines to connect words, phrases, or examples together.
Remember, you are encouraged to use pictures, words, phrases,
or any other representation. Be creative and make it your own
interpretation of the information. Take about five minutes to
make your mind map. Please begin.

Teacher waits approximately five minutes for students to complete the task.

To further encourage students' activation of prior knowledge, while at the same time deepening their understanding of the knowledge, take the mind mapping activity a step further. Have students select several words, phrases, or examples that they have linked together and write a complete sentence containing those words, phrases, or examples. For example, a student may have linked the term "commutative property" with the words "addition" and "multiplication." A sentence linking these words would be "The commutative property applies to the operations of addition and multiplication."

> ### Stop-n-Think Box 3.4
>
> Let's give you a head start by creating an example of a mind map for your classroom.
>
> 1. Select a concept or big idea from your content area and grade level (e.g., Newton's Laws of Motion, salinity, natural selection, right triangle trigonometry, systems of inequalities).
>
> 2. Brainstorm a list of words, phrases, or examples associated with your concept or big idea.
>
> 3. Create a mind map from your list, starting with a circle in the middle of the page that is about the size of an egg yolk.
>
> 4. Finally, create three or more sentences that explain the links between words, phrases, or examples in your mind map.
>
> Now you have an example to share with your class.

How Gossip Makes for Better Learning

John Medina's best-selling book *Brain Rules* (2008) organizes an incredibly robust amount of research on the brain and learning into 12 basic rules. One of those rules highlights the importance of talking and sharing what we know with someone else. Those of us who have spent longer than two seconds in a middle school or high school are quite familiar with teenage gossip. In fact, this contagious act engages even the most mature science and mathematics teachers by satisfying a repressed desire to hear what someone else knows that we may not know. One major characteristic of gossip is that it sticks and is rarely forgotten, even in the face of rebuttals and refuting evidence. Wouldn't it be nice if we could channel this fascination with gossip into something that would activate prior knowledge? Believe it or not, the answer is that we can take advantage of gossip.

One of the most effective ways to move something from short-term memory into long-term memory is to tell someone what we know (Bahrick, 2000; Hasher & Zacks, 1984a, 1984b; Peterson & Peterson, 1959; Squire, 2004; Squire & Kandel, 1999). In other words, talk it out. In addition to the emotional component, gossip sticks around because it is repeated verbally (Medina, 2008). So, how can we use this to our advantage? A turn-to!

A turn-to is a strategy that simply asks students to "turn to" their neighbors or folks close by and do something. That something, in this case, is talk to their neighbors about their prior knowledge. Take the brainstorming and mind mapping activity that we have developed in this chapter. Having students turn to their neighbor and explain their mind maps or read their connecting sentences offers them an opportunity to "gossip" about knowledge. As teachers engage students in these types of follow-up conversations, it is often beneficial to give them advance notice of this expectation. Make them aware that after they "gossip," read, discuss, or observe a piece of information, they will be expected to "say something." This response may be shared in the form of making a prediction, asking a question, clarifying something they are thinking about, or just making a simple comment. In the end, they stand a better chance of remembering the information, something we will find incredibly valuable for the day's lesson (Bahrick, 2000; Hasher & Zacks, 1984a, 1984b; LeDoux, 2002; Squire, 2004).

Stand Up–Hand Up–Pair Up

Teacher: *Please stand up, walk across the room, give someone a high five, and pair up with that person. Join up with another pair and arrange yourselves in groups of four.*

Teacher pauses and waits for students to arrange themselves in groups. Instruct students to sit at desks, if necessary.

Teacher: *Great. Within your groups, please number off, starting with 1, so that someone in your group is 1, someone is 2, and so on.*

Teacher pauses and waits for students to number off.

Teacher: *Please pause where you are. If you are a 1, hold up one finger. If you are a 2, hold up two fingers. If you are a 3, hold up three fingers.*

The Teacher checks to make sure everyone has a number.

Teacher: *Thank you, you can relax your hands. Starting with 1, take turns describing and explaining your mind map to the other group members. Each group member has approximately two minutes.*

The time is on the board.

Before we start, turn to your group members and say, "Let's do it."

Go.

Teacher walks around the room and listens in on the conversations.

Did you ever notice how some students tend to drift off during group work? As teachers increase their use of cooperative learning and student-centered learning, it is important to structure the experience so all students are contributing to the experience and are held accountable for doing some part of the work. At the conclusion of the preceding vignette, select several students to summarize what they learned from other members in their group. Using a spinner, preselected playing cards, or a die, have each group member with the corresponding number stand up and share his or her summarizing thoughts. Adding this type of discussion to the end of the activity will increase the probability that students will stay on task during the group discussion.

A Golden Oldie: The KWL Chart

Every now and then you just have to clean out the cabinets, closets, and drawers. As you dig through the stash of items that are being exposed to the light of day for the first time in a long while, nostalgia sets in as you recall the stories and memories from days gone by. Although this cleaning out of cabinets, closets, and drawers is not on my list of things to do for fun, the discovery of a rare gem that has withstood the test of time makes it all worth it: a golden oldie. Something I can still use! For activating prior knowledge, this golden oldie is the KWL Chart.

"K"—What you already know	"W"—What you want to know (i.e., questions)	"L"—What you have learned

Typically, the KWL Chart is a three-column graphic organizer. Students fill in the column on the far left with things they know about a particular topic (the *K*). The middle column is reserved for things the students want to know about that same topic (the *W*). Finally, the column on the far right is filled in at the end of the teaching episode with things the students have learned (the *L*). This can be done as a class, or each student can complete his or her own KWL Chart. Either way, this graphic organizer provides a means for activating prior knowledge and setting learning goals and a means of assessment, which are discussed in later chapters. Now let's take this golden oldie and put a new twist on the strategy in a manner fitting with the recipe framework of this book.

As students arrive to class, provide them with a pad of sticky notes. Once they are in their seats, settling down, and curious about the sticky notes, show them the poster-size KWL Chart you have inconspicuously hung up behind the projector screen.

> Teacher: *Good afternoon. Raise your hand if you are wondering why I handed you a pad of sticky notes as you arrived to class.*
>
> Teacher waits for students to raise hand or look at him or her with confusion.
>
> Teacher: *Today's topic is the electrical circuit. What do you already know about circuits? As you think about what you already know about circuits, write each thought down on a sticky note and stick it to your desk. Each time you think of something, it gets its own sticky note. Let's see if you can use seven or eight sticky notes. You have 1 minute and 45 seconds.*
>
> *Go.*
>
> Teacher wanders around the room, observing students filing out their sticky notes and offering help to those who may be stuck.

Once students have had a chance to brainstorm with the sticky notes, it is time to place these nuggets of prior knowledge onto the class KWL Chart. The procedure for doing this will be up to you and the personality of the class. One approach is for the teacher to place the sticky notes on the chart one by one as the students verbally share each new idea. Another approach is to have the students walk up and place their notes on the chart as a way to get them out of their desks.

> Teacher: *In about 10 seconds, when I say go, walk up and place your sticky notes under the letter* K.
>
> *Go.*
>
> Teacher observes students placing their sticky notes under the letter *K* while the *William Tell Overture* plays on the compact disc player.

Once students have returned to their seats, have them make their own KWL Chart and fill in the ideas that were generated on the poster-size chart. The other two columns of this graphic organizer, the *W* and the *L*, are very important as well and should be used as you move through teaching the lesson or unit. Have your students file away their KWL Charts and revisit them later in the lesson on electrical circuits.

It's All in How You Ask the Question

Teachers often use thought-provoking questions to activate their students' prior knowledge (Dantonio & Beisenherz, 2001; King, 1994). Let's reflect and examine your thoughts about the questions you ask your students.

> **Stop-n-Think Box 3.5**
>
> Make a list of all the reasons you ask students questions.

So why do you ask your students questions? Review the list you just generated for Stop-n-Think Box 3.5. Do you notice any trends in the reasons for asking students questions? Are your questions for eliciting, probing, and extending student thinking? Do your questions seek student opinion on particular topics? Are your questions an evaluation or assessment of student understanding? Have you ever found yourself asking a student a question because a particular student was not paying attention? Believe me; you are not alone in the *gotcha* purpose for asking a question. Teachers often use questions as a classroom management strategy, to get the attention of a disengaged student. Together with the type of question, the reason for asking a particular question in class has a strong association with both student engagement and the activation of prior knowledge.

A question can be either open or closed. The reason for a question can be to elicit, probe, or extend student thinking and ideas. Questioning, as a specific strategy for engagement, will appear again in subsequent chapters. However, with respect to the activation prior knowledge, let's look closer at open versus closed questions and questions for eliciting and probing student thinking.

Open Versus Closed Questions

In general, there are two types of question: open and closed (Allen, 2001; Boaler, 1998; Dohrenwend, 1965). The salient difference between these two broad categories of questions is the type of thinking involved in responding to an open versus a closed question. Consider the following two questions: What is the best way to solve a system of inequalities? and Given a system of inequalities, what are your ideas on how to solve the system? Now consider a science example: What is the most important difference between a transverse wave and a longitudinal wave? and What are some differences between a transverse wave and a longitudinal wave? Semantically, the difference between these questions is subtle. Cognitively, the difference is the decision of the student to engage or not to engage. For both the mathematics and the science example, the first question is a closed question and the second an open question. The words *best* and *most important* close the responses down to one acceptable answer. The exchange of these words in the second questions for phrases like *your ideas* and *some differences* opens the question up for multiple acceptable answers. Why is this seemingly minor difference such a big deal for engagement?

Imagine for a moment that you are 16 years old and occupy a seat in a high school physics classroom. The teacher has announced that class will begin with a review of yesterday's material. Here comes the question: What is the most important difference between a transverse wave and a longitudinal wave? The phrasing of this question, specifically the use of the phrase *most important*, triggers a response in the student brain that often discourages engagement. Here is how this response goes. First, the student brain must thumb through the collection of thoughts and memories associated with both transverse and longitudinal waves. This may take some time. Then the student brain must sort this collection of thoughts and memories into a two mental piles: things associated with a transverse wave and things associated with longitudinal wave. After comparing and contrasting these two mental heaps and making a mental list of their differences, the student brain must select the *most important* one. Up until this point, the student is more than likely cognitively engaged as he or she completes the preceding mental tasks. However, one final step is left in processing a response to this seemingly harmless question for activating prior knowledge. The student brain must ask, "Is the most important difference on my list the same as the most important difference on the teacher's list?" To avoid being wrong and saving face with his or her peers, the student will probably not respond or not volunteer to engage in this activation of prior knowledge all because the teacher asked a closed question. When asking a closed question, the teacher is subconsciously signaling to the students that only one response will qualify as an acceptable response and thus requires convergent thinking. Convergent thinking is associated with the development of a single answer with no room for ambiguity (Runco & Acar, 2012). For students developing an understanding of a concept in science and mathematics, this can be disengaging (Allen, 2001).

On the flip side of the scenario described, adjusting this question about mechanical waves to a more open question eliminates the internal tug-of-war between the brain and student engagement. What if the teacher had first asked students to brainstorm a list of characteristics or features associated with transverse waves and then, after some time, asked students to brainstorm a separate list of characteristics or feature associated with longitudinal waves? As open questions, these two tasks encourage divergent thinking, which subconsciously signals to students that there is a collection of responses that qualify as acceptable responses. Divergent thinking is associated with creative thinking and the opportunity to explore a variety of outcomes (Runco & Acar, 2012). For students developing an understanding of a concept in science and mathematics, this approach provides a safe environment in which they can explore and share their thinking without the fear of not selecting the single correct or acceptable answer. This is safer and more engaging (Allen, 2001). From a teacher's perspective, the number of student responses will increase simply because it is a safer activation of prior knowledge that encourages a variety of responses.

Teacher: *Good morning class. Please get out something to write with and something to write on.*

Teacher waits for students to get out the requested materials.

Teacher: *Divide your sheet of paper into two columns. On the top of one column put the words "transverse waves" and on the top of the second column put the words "longitudinal waves."*

Teacher pauses and waits for students to prepare the columns.

Teacher: *Take two or three minutes and fill in everything you remember about transverse waves in the transverse waves column and everything you remember about longitudinal waves in the longitudinal waves column.*

Teacher waits for several minutes as students fill in their charts. The teacher may move throughout the room to gauge when students are out of ideas and ready to move on.

Teacher: *Great. Now turn to a neighbor and compare lists. Add or change items as you and your neighbor share lists. Go!*

Teacher pauses to allow this discussion to take place. Again, move throughout the room to gauge when partners are wrapping up their discussions.

Teacher: *Please end your discussions and say thank you to your neighbor for chatting. Today's opening question is, how are transverse and longitudinal waves different? Using your newly created lists for both types of waves, circle, underline, or highlight a couple of differences you notice between the two lists. Go!*

Teacher waits for students to complete this task and then asks them to share.

One way to know whether your questions are open or closed is to examine your questions through the lens of high consensus versus low consensus. If we want students to engage in divergent thoughts, when every student is thinking independently, then we are encouraging student responses to have low consensus, that is, more than one answer. In the preceding example, asking students to identify the best way and the most important difference is communicating to students that there is one correct response. This type of response requires a high level of consensus. If we truly want to promote open-ended thinking, we must word our questions in a way that facilitates low-consensus student responses. Too often, teachers avoid these types of open-ended, thought-provoking questions due to the length of time it takes for students to respond. Don't let that prevent you from asking effective questions.

There is a time and place for closed questioning. Once students have had the opportunity to activate their prior knowledge, closed questioning can then be implemented to fine-tune their understanding of a concept or topic. The preceding vignette uses a series of open-ended questions to draw out students' prior knowledge of the two concepts. This example is in stark contrast to a teacher standing up in front of the room and saying, "Today we are continuing our discussion of mechanical waves. Who can tell me the difference between transverse and longitudinal waves?" Odds are that this approach will be met by silence and stares. The activation of prior knowledge is a gradual process that starts with divergent thinking and progresses toward convergent thinking. Reversing this process by starting with a closed question can disengage learners at the beginning of class period, with little chance of getting them back. Let's look at a mathematics example.

Teacher: *Welcome back. Today we are going to explore solving systems of three inequalities. Please get out something to write with and a blank sheet of paper.*

Teacher waits for students to get out the requested materials.

Teacher: *At the top of that sheet of paper, write the phrase "solving inequalities."*

Teacher pauses and waits for students to write the phrase.

Teacher: *I have placed an example of an inequality on the board. On your sheet of paper, please develop a list of written instructions you would use to solve the inequality.*

Teacher waits for several minutes as students write out their instructions. The teacher may move throughout the room to gauge when students are out of ideas and ready to move on.

Teacher: *Great. Now look at the example of a system of inequalities on the board. On your sheet of paper, please develop a list of written instructions you would use to solve the system. Feel free to refer your book or notes for ideas.*

Teacher waits for several minutes as students write out their instructions. The teacher may move throughout the room to gauge when students are out of ideas and ready to move on.

Teacher: *Great. Now turn to a neighbor and compare instructions. Add or change items as you and your neighbor share your responses. Go!*

Teacher pauses to allow this discussion to take place. Again, the teacher moves throughout the room to gauge when partners are wrapping up their discussions.

Teacher: *Please end your discussions and say thank you to your neighbor for chatting. Today's topic requires us to know how to solve systems of inequalities. How did your approach differ from your neighbor's approach? Circle, underline, or highlight a couple of differences you notice between the two sets of instructions. Go!*

Teacher waits for students to complete this task and then asks them to share. At this time, the teacher may decide to work through the examples using student ideas.

Stop-n-Think Box 3.6

Reflect on a specific lesson or class period. What are some specific examples of questions that your recall asking your students?

Which questions were open questions, and which questions were closed? How could you change a closed question to an open question?

Finally, does the phrasing of your questions align with your purpose for asking them? How can you edit them to focus on eliciting and probing student thinking?

Link to the Recipe for Engagement

In today's science and mathematics classrooms, when instructional time is at a premium, the activation of prior knowledge is an issue of effectiveness and efficiency. The role of activating prior knowledge, or priming the brain, is much like the beginning stages of using any recipe: You have to prepare before beginning to cook. If you are going to make a steaming pot of homemade vegetable soup, cooking will be much more efficient if you prepare all the necessary ingredients and seasonings before starting. Running back and forth to the vegetable drawer to gather, clean, slice, and chop each item separately will result in a frustrating and time-consuming experience. The same idea applies to the learning of content in science and mathematics. Before teachers can successfully orchestrate and implement an effective learning experience for students, some prep time is needed. This prep time is not about a planning period. Instead, the preparation here is the teacher's conscious decision to activate the students' prior knowledge through specific and targeted strategies. Teachers must first identify the ingredients with which they will be working in class and get them ready. Activating the prior knowledge of students with the strategies presented in this chapter before diving into content makes for more effective and efficient instructional time. Prime the brain!

CHAPTER 3: FIST LIST EXIT TICKET

A "fist list" is a summarizing strategy that asks students, or readers, to identify five major points or ideas from an activity, discussion, or reading. As students develop their lists of major points or ideas, they keep count with their fingers (see Figures 3.2). These major points or ideas can be facts, applications, or evaluative comments about the material. The goal is to list at least five points or ideas.

Photo from Thinkstock.com.

Figure 3.2   A Fist List

After reading this chapter, develop a "fist list" of the major ideas or concepts about activating prior knowledge. Jot down the items on your fist list.

1. _____

2. _____

3. _____

4. _____

5. _____

An extension of this Exit Ticket would be to make one fist list that contains essential points and ideas within this chapter and then create a second fist list focusing on an application of those points or ideas to your life or classroom.

Engaging Professional Development Tasks

1. This professional development task encourages you to develop a set of questions that you might use during one of your instructional lessons and then predict students' responses. While developing your lesson plan for an upcoming class, write out the questions you will use to activate prior knowledge. Although this will feel awkward at first, developing and rehearsing the questions you plan to ask will make your approach to questioning for prior knowledge more purposeful and effective. Then, check your list of questions to see whether they are open or closed. Reflect on the following questions:

   - Do your questions elicit, probe, or extend student thinking?
   - Do the questions align with what you want going on in your students' mind?
   - Have you developed a variety of questions that activate your students' prior knowledge?
   - Does the type of questions provide you with the important and necessary information you are trying to obtain about your students and their thinking?
   - Are your questions appropriate for the content of the lesson? For example, if you are asking them how to solve a system of equations using elimination, would you want to use an open or closed question? Maybe you are asking your students to chart the pathway of blood through the heart. Would you select the language of an open or closed

question? It is important that your questions match what you want going on in the minds of your learners. If you are asking them to brainstorm ways to solve systems of equations or identify the characteristics of the circulatory system, you will probably want several open-ended questions that probe and extend students' thinking.

2. The second part of this professional development experience is the prediction of student responses. For each question you developed, predict and write down all the possible answers that these questions might generate. Write down your anticipated student responses for each specific question. Then ask yourself, "What responses am I really looking for? What misconceptions am I interested in uncovering?" This prediction exercise will become a guide for you as you assess and respond to students' answers and guide their ability to activate prior knowledge. In addition, anticipating or predicting student responses allows for better preparation for where to go next.

3. This professional development task encourages you to assemble a set of "classroom activators." Using your ideas and strategies along with ideas and strategies from your colleagues, compile a list of ways to activate prior knowledge in your class. Keep these ideas general and not content specific. For example, "make a concept map of yesterday's topic." Put each idea on a separate index card, and ask your media center specialist to laminate the cards. The goal here is to have enough index cards so that every student can have one. Put these cards in a box or a basket somewhere in your classroom. When students enter the classroom, have them draw a card from the box or basket and complete the activator described on their card. After students have completed the activator individually, have students turn to their neighbors and share their work. This opening activity provides students with a way to activate prior knowledge and offers a variety of ways for doing it.

References

Alexander, P. A., Kulikowich, J. M., & Schulze, S. K. (1994). How subject-matter knowledge affects recall and interest. *American Educational Research Journal, 31*(2), 313–337.

Allen, R. H. (2001). *Impact teaching: Ideas and strategies for teachers to maximize student learning.* Boston: Allyn & Bacon.

Alvermann, D. (1981). The compensatory effect of graphic organizers on descriptive texts. *Journal of Educational Research, 75,* 44–48.

Anderson, J. R. (1983). *The architecture of cognition.* Cambridge, MA: Harvard University Press.

Ausubel, D. P. (1968). *Educational psychology: A cognitive view.* New York: Holt, Rinehart & Winston.

Bahrick, H. P. (2000). Long-term maintenance of knowledge. In E. Tulving & F. I. M. Craik (Eds.), *The Oxford handbook of memory* (pp. 347–362). New York: Oxford Press.

Boaler, J. (1998). Open and closed mathematics: Student experiences and understandings. *Journal for Research in Mathematics Education, 29*(1), 41–62.

Buckner, R. L., Koutstaal, W., Schacter, D. L., & Rosen, B. R. (2000). Functional MRI evidence for a role of frontal and inferior temporal cortex in amodal components of priming. *Brain, 123,* 620–640.

Buckner, R. L., Petersen, S. E., Ojemann, J. G., Miezin, F. M., Squire, L. R., & Raichle, M. E. (1995). Functional anatomical studies of explicit and implicit memory retrieval tasks. *Journal of Neuroscience, 15,* 12–29.

Dantonio, M., & Beisenherz, P. (2001). *Learning to question, questioning to learn.* Boston: Allyn & Bacon.

DeWitt, M. R., Knight, J. B., Hicks, J. L., & Ball, B. H. (2012). The effects of prior knowledge on the encoding of episodic contextual details. *Psychonomic Bulletin Review, 19,* 251–257.

Dohrenwend, B. S. (1965). Some effects of open and closed questions on respondents' answers. *Human Organization, 24*(2), 175–184.

Durso, F. T., & Coggins, K. A. (1991). Organized instruction for the improvement of word knowledge skills. *Journal of Educational Psychology, 83*(1), 108–112.

Estes, T. H., Mills, D. C., & Barron, R. F. (1969). Three methods of introducing students to a reading-learning task in two content subjects. In H. L. Herber & P. L. Sanders (Eds.), *Research in reading in the content areas: First year report* (pp. 40–47). Syracuse, NY: Syracuse University Press.

Foos, P. W. (1995). The effect of variations in text summarization opportunities on test performance. *Journal of Experimental Education, 63,* 89–95.

Griffin, M. M., & Robinson, D. H. (2005). Does spatial or visual information in maps facilitate text recall? Reconsidering the conjoint retention hypothesis. *Educational Technology Research and Development, 53,* 23–36.

Hasher, L., & Zacks, R. T. (1984a). Automatic and effortful processes in memory. *Journal of Experimental Psychology, 198,* 356–388.

Hasher, L., & Zacks, R. T. (1984b). Automatic processing of fundamental information: The case for frequency of occurrence. *American Psychologist, 39,* 1372–1388.

Holliday, W. G., Brunner, L. L., & Donais, E. L. (1977). Differential cognitive and affective responses to flow diagrams in science. *Journal of Research in Science Teaching, 14,* 129–138.

Horton, P. B., McConney, A. A., Gallo, M., Woods, A. L., Senn, G. J., & Hamelin, D. (1993). An investigation of the effectiveness of concept mapping as an instructional tool. *Science Education, 77,* 95–111.

Ives, B., & Hoy, C. (2003). Graphic organizers applied to higher-level secondary mathematics. *Learning Disabilities Research & Practice, 18*, 36–51.

King, A. (1994). Guiding knowledge construction in the classroom: Effects of teaching children how to question and how to explain. *American Educational Research Journal, 31*(2), 338–368.

Laroche, S., Davis, S., & Jay, T. M. (2000). Plasticity at hippocampal to prefrontal cortex synapses: Dual roles in working memory and consolidation. *Hippocampus, 10*, 438–446.

LeDoux, J. (2002). *Synaptic self: How our brains become who we are.* New York: Viking Press.

Manns, J. R., Hopkins, R. O., & Squire, L. R. (2003). Semantic memory and the human hippocampus. *Neuron, 38*, 127–133.

Mayer, R. E. (1989). Systematic thinking fostered by illustrations in scientific text. *Journal of Educational Psychology, 81*, 240–246.

Medina, J. (2008). *Brain rules. 12 principles for surviving and thriving at work, home, and school.* Seattle, WA: Pear Press.

Miller, G. A. (1956). The magical number seven, plus or minus two: Some limits on our capacity for processing information. *The Psychological Review, 63*(2), 81–97.

Nesbit, J. C., & Adesope, O. O. (2006). Learning with concept and knowledge maps: A meta-analysis. *Review of Educational Research, 76*(3), 413–448.

Novak, J. D., & Gowin, D. B. (1984). *Learning how to learn.* New York: Cambridge University Press.

O'Donnell, A. M., Dansereau, D. F., & Hall, R. H. (2002). Knowledge maps as scaffolds for cognitive processing. *Educational Psychology Review, 14*, 71–86.

Ormrod, J. E. (2011). *Human learning* (6th ed.). Upper Saddle River, NJ: Prentice Hall.

Patterson, M. E., Dansereau, D. F., & Wiegmann, D. A. (1993) Receiving information during a cooperative episode: Effects of communication aids and verbal ability. *Learning and Individual Differences 5*, 1–11.

Peterson, L. R., & Peterson, M. J. (1959). Short-term retention of individual verbal items. *Journal of Experimental Psychology, 58*, 193–198.

Raichle, M. E., Fiez, J. A., Videen, T. O., MacLeod, A. M., Pardo, J. V., Fox, P. T., & Petersen, S. E. (1994). Practice-related changes in human brain functional anatomy during nonmotor learning. *Cerebral Cortex, 4*, 8–26.

Runco, M. A., & Acar, S. (2012). Divergent thinking as an indicator of creative potential. *Creativity Research Journal, 24*(1), 66–75.

Schacter, D. L., & Buckner, R. L. (1998). Priming and the brain. *Neuron, 20*, 185–195.

Schacter, D. L., Dobbins, I. G., & Schnyer, D. M. (2004). Specificity of priming: A cognitive neuroscience perspective. *Nature Reviews Neuroscience, 5*, 853–862.

Schacter, D. L., Wig, G. S., & Stevens, W. D. (2007). Reductions in cortical activity during priming. *Current Opinion in Neurobiology, 17*, 171–176.

Schneider, W. (1993). Domain-specific knowledge and memory performance in children. *Educational Psychology Review, 5*, 257–273.

Sousa, D. A. (2011). *How the brain learns* (4th ed.). Thousand Oaks, CA: Corwin.

Squire, L. R. (1992). Memory and the hippocampus: A synthesis from findings with rats, monkeys, and humans. *Psychological Review, 99*(2), 195–231.

Squire, L. R. (2004). Memory systems of the brain: A brief history and current perspective. *Neurobiology of Learning and Memory, 82,* 171–177.

Squire, L. R., & Kandel, E. R. (1999). *Memory: From mind to molecules.* New York: Scientific American Library.

Squire, L. R., Ojemann, J. G., Miezin, F. M., Petersen, S. E., Videen, T. O., & Raichle, M. E. (1992). Activation of the hippocampus in normal humans: A functional anatomical study of memory. *Proceedings of the National Academy of Sciences, USA, 89,* 1837–1841.

Stensvold, M. S., & Wilson, J. T. (1990). The interaction of verbal ability with concept mapping in learning from a chemistry laboratory activity. *Science Education, 74,* 473– 480.

Sylwester, R. (2005). *How to explain a brain. An educator's handbook of brain terms and cognitive processes.* Thousand Oaks, CA: Corwin.

Tobias, S. (1994). Interest, prior knowledge, and learning. *Review of Educational Research, 63,* 37–54.

Tulving, E., & Schacter, D. L. (1990). Priming and human memory systems. *Science, 247,* 301–306.

Wagner, A. D., Desmond, J. E., Demb, J. B., Glover, D. H., & Gabrieli, J. D. E. (1997). Semantic repetition priming for verbal and pictorial knowledge: A functional MRI study of the left inferior prefrontal cortex. *Journal of Cognitive Neuroscience, 9,* 714–726.

Wig, G. S., Buckner, R. L., & Schacter, D. L. (2009). Repetition priming influences distinct brain systems: Evidence from task-evoked data and resting-state correlations. *Journal of Neurophysiology, 101,* 2632–2648.

Willingham, D., & Daniel, D. (2012). Teaching to what students have in common. *Educational Leadership, 69*(5), 16–21.

Winn, W. (1991). Learning from maps and diagrams. *Educational Psychology Review, 3,* 211–247.

4

Captivate With Novelty

K eeping with the "recipe for engagement" theme, the human palate prefers a little seasoning on most of the food that we ingest. A clear liquid diet or bland foods are rarely preferred over a nicely seasoned piece of Atlantic salmon or perfectly marinated cut of filet mignon. For vegetarians, a dish of steaming hot eggplant parmesan with chunks of tomato and the aroma of oregano will certainly sate an appetite. On the contrary, an over-seasoned piece of meat or steamed vegetables weighed down by too much salt and pepper can force us to leave our plates virtually untouched and give us a strong desire to get up from the table and walk away. Let's examine this same scenario, only the food in this case represents the content in a particular lesson we are serving to our science and mathematics students on a daily basis. If the content or topic of the day is bland with no hint of seasoning, students will most likely not engage; they certainly will not ingest the material and will mentally get up and walk away. Likewise, if the classroom is peppered with too much seasoning so that the students find it virtually impossible to discern the content from the chaos, students will also not engage, not ingest, and most likely mentally get up and walk away. The difference lies in what we as teachers use as seasoning. Seasoning, in this case, is the use of novelty. And like seasoning, too much or too little will not be appetizing to the student. As teachers, we strive for the amount of novelty to be "just right" (Wolfe, 2010).

We are often taught that classroom management is based on safe, predictable routines because students need to know what to expect. Some would say that a lack of predictability has the potential to cause classroom disruption. However, too much predictability can be boring. So, if novelty is about creating learning in unique ways and predictability is important to maintain an effective learning environment, when is novelty effective?

Stop-n-Think Box 4.1

What role does novelty play in your classroom? How do you recognize novelty?

What does novelty look like?	What does novelty sound like?

If novelty is used to capture your student's attention, make a list of the strategies you currently use that add novelty to your lessons.

Using the responses you provided in Stop-n-Think Box 4.1, let's take a look at how the brains of your students respond to novelty and why they crave just the right amount of "seasoning" in each and every lesson. To do this, you will need to hypothesize the connection between venetian blinds, a smoke detector, Yahoo!, a chief executive, and a personal liaison.

In the Classroom, Novelty Is the Spice of Life

Novelty in the classroom captivates the student brain—well, any brain for that matter—by activating several areas and a certain chemical of the brain responsible for attention and focus (McGaugh, 2004; Nieoullon & Coquerel, 2003; Posner & Dehaene, 1994; Raz & Buhle, 2006). The areas are the reticular activating system, the prefrontal cortex, the amygdala, and the cingulate gyrus, and the chemical is the neurotransmitter dopamine (Posner & Dehaene, 1994; Posner & Peterson, 1990). Each of these brain areas are involved in captivating the attention of your students and, more important, helping them to decide what to pay attention to and what to disregard as irrelevant stimuli. If you are curious about the novel list of items provided in the previous section (i.e., venetian blinds, a smoke detector, Yahoo!, a chief executive, and a personal liaison), let's clear that up now. Each of these items is analogous to the areas and chemical of the brain associated with attention and focus.

The Reticular Activating System

The reticular activating system, or RAS, acts like the venetian blinds for the brain. Just as venetian blinds can be opened or closed to let sunlight in, an activated RAS controls the brain's response level to stimuli. The RAS is a collection of neurons in the lower, back part of the brain that alert us to stimuli to which we do or do not attend (see Figure 4.1; Friedenberg & Silverman, 2012).

In other words, when the RAS is activated and working efficiently, it helps your students separate stimuli that are relevant from stimuli that are irrelevant (Willis, 2006; Wolfe, 2010). For a classroom teacher, this is extraordinarily helpful. As teachers, we ask students to attend to stimuli in the classroom by providing activities centered on the topic or content of the lesson. At the same time, we are competing against irrelevant stimuli such as afterschool events, personal issues, the hum of the projector, the sound of the heating or air-conditioning

Figure 4.1   Brain With RAS

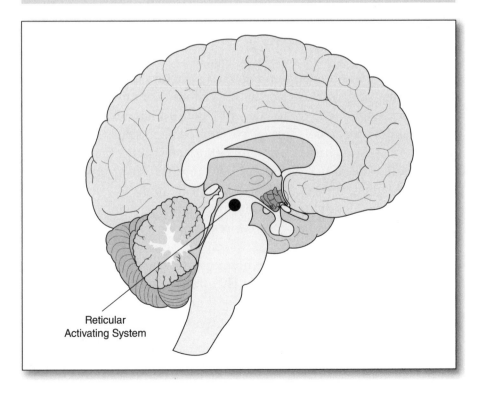

Reticular
Activating System

unit, or students passing by outside of the classroom door or window. On most days, this can be an uphill battle. As a teenager, are you going to be more interested in the angle-side-angle postulate for proving congruency or the Friday night football game and the social plans surrounding the game? This answer is a given.

So how do we address this issue in the classroom? The answer to this question is in the title of this chapter: novelty. In addition to survival and choice, novelty is associated with the arousal of the RAS (Raz & Buhle, 2006; Shirey, 1992). When tasks are routine, the RAS is less active and diminishes our ability to decide what to attend to and what to ignore. It is in this brain situation that our students are more likely to attend to something that is irrelevant than to the task at hand. However, when a task is novel, the RAS becomes more active and increases our ability to decide what to attend to and what to ignore. If the novelty is associated with the topic or content of the lesson, our students are more likely to attend to the lesson (Braver, Reynolds, & Donaldson, 2003; Raz & Buhle, 2006).

The Amazing Amygdala

Once a novel task has stimulated the RAS, the brain signals the sensory neurons to take in the collection of stimuli associated with that particular task. In other words, "Pay attention!" However, as part of our survival system, the brain has a structure that determines whether the novel task that just grabbed our attention is or is not a life-or-death situation that requires the fight or flight response. Meet your amazing amygdala (see Figure 4.2).

The amygdala is an almond-shaped structure found at the end of both the left and right hippocampi. A more thorough discussion of the hippocampus will come later, but you do have bilateral hippocampi and amygdalae. This dopamine-packed structure found in your limbic system has the very important task of checking all incoming stimuli, especially novel stimuli, for uncertainty or unknown factors and making the decision about fight or flight (Gonen, Admon, Podlipsky, & Hendler, 2012; Harmon-Jones & van Honk, 2012; Lindquist, Wager, Kober, Bliss-Moreau, & Barrett, 2012). It is the amygdala's role in sounding the alarm for fight or flight that likens the amygdala to the brain's own smoke detector. When the smoke detector goes off, a flood of brain chemicals is released into the system to send the body into fight-or-flight mode. In addition, the amygdala releases dopamine into the brain so that the brain can better remember this amygdala-alerting, alarm-sounding experience and

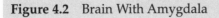

Figure 4.2   Brain With Amygdala

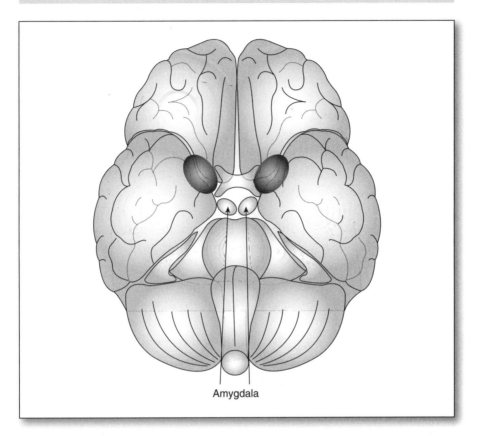

Amygdala

avoid it in the future (Cahill, Babinsky, Markowitsch, & McGaugh, 1995; Cahill & McGaugh, 1998; LeDoux, 1996, 2002; Nieoullon & Coquerel, 2003). However, this analogy leaves out an additional function of the amygdala: the function that teachers can take advantage of each and every day in our classrooms.

Dopamine

The amygdala is also involved in the processing of emotions, both positive and negative (Breiter et al., 1996; Hennenlotter et al., 2005; Somerville, Kim, Johnstone, Alexander, & Whalen, 2004). When the amygdala processes an emotional event, it also releases a surge of dopamine into the brain (Cahill & McGaugh, 1995; Nieoullon & Coquerel, 2003). Dopamine is a neurotransmitter that is associated with memory retention and information processing (Berry, Cervantes-Sandoval, Nicholas, & Davis, 2012; Schicknick et al., 2012; Whalley, 2012). Memory retention and information processing are two processes that are very important in our science and mathematics classrooms. When dopamine surges in the brain, it triggers feelings of euphoria and the desire to yell, "Yahoo!" (Jensen, 2005). Studies strongly suggest that when the brain is enriched with a bath of dopamine, working memory capacity increases, mood regulation improves, and memory retention goes up (Berry et al., 2012; Schicknick et al., 2012; Whalley, 2012). John Medina (2008) likens this function of the amygdala to using sticky notes on experiences. Just as you and I use sticky notes to help us remember things, when an experience and the accompanying stimuli include high emotional content—positive or negative—the amygdala places a dopamine sticky note on the experience so that the brain will flag the experience for later recall (Dolcos, LaBar, & Cabeza, 2004).

Take a minute to identify and think about the best vacation you have ever experienced. In contrast, think about the worse vacation you have ever experienced. How long did it take you to remember those events? In most cases, the memories will come to your mind rather quickly because those events are emotional events. Students' ability to retain information will increase when there is an emotional connection. Novelty is positive emotional content.

> ## Stop-n-Think Box 4.2
>
> Summarize the importance of the amygdala in classroom learning. How is this understanding of the amygdala as a sticky note important in your classroom?

The Cingulate Gyrus and Prefrontal Cortex

Now that the RAS and the amygdala are responding to the novel experience, the brain must call on two higher-order processing centers to incorporate this novel experience into memory and find a place to store it. These two areas are the cingulate gyrus and prefrontal cortex (PFC; see Figure 4.3).

Located smack dab in the middle of the cortex, the cingulate gyrus is the personal liaison between the emotional, often irrational, parts of the brain and the area of the brain responsible for executive functioning (Friedenberg & Silverman, 2012; Ripke et al., in press). As the personal liaison, the cingulate gyrus listens to the emotional component of the experience provided by the amygdala and other members of the limbic system and communicates this information to the PFC, the chief executive (Friedenberg & Silverman, 2012).

Figure 4.3   Brain With Cingulate Gyrus and Prefrontal Cortex

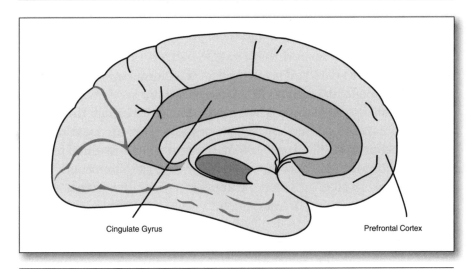

Cingulate Gyrus   Prefrontal Cortex

Source: Adapted from Mysid Brodmann/Wikipedia.

The teenage brain is going through a significant developmental growth spurt (Wolfe, 2010). As a result, the chief executive, or PFC, is often out to lunch. The symptoms of this include inability to identify and manage emotions, lack of forward thinking or planning, the inability to make decisions, seeking novelty without the ability to process it, and difficulty in processing higher-order thinking (Blakemore, 2008, 2012; Blakemore & Choudhury, 2006; Wolfe, 2010). In other words, teenagers often cave to their emotions without making use of the brain's personal liaison, the cingulate gyrus. As a result, classrooms with teenagers require specific strategies that help to improve communication between the emotional systems and the higher-order processing systems (Choudhury, 2010; Crawford, 2007; Feinstein, 2009; Wolfe, 2010). Upcoming chapters discuss specific strategies for facilitating this process. But suffice it to say, we have to provide an environment with enough novelty to capture the teenage brain's attention.

In Need of an Antacid Tablet?

Picture it: Room 219, eighth-grade science, and the topic is air pressure. Adolescents file into Mr. Smith's classroom, take their assigned seats, and get out their textbooks, science notebooks, and a writing utensil. Mr. Smith informs the students, "Today we are learning about air pressure." He asks the students to open their textbooks to page 145 and randomly selects a name from the name cards stacked on his desk. This student is then asked to start reading the section aloud while his or her classmates follow along. After a time, Mr. Smith selects a second name and that student picks up reading where the previous student paused. This process of selecting names and reading aloud continues until the class has read the entire section on air pressure. You know where this story is going. The students are then asked to write down the definitions of the vocabulary words from the section and to answer the questions at the end of the reading in their science notebooks. What is not finished in class is to be completed at home. There is little doubt that the announcement that science is over for the day is met with much relief from the eighth graders in Mr. Smith's class.

This is not a story to pick on Mr. Smith, or any male science teacher for that matter. Believe it or not, this approach to teaching science is not uncommon in classrooms all over the country, regardless of the gender of the teacher (Banilower, Smith, Weiss, & Pasley, 2006). The point to the story is what this read-aloud exercise did for the brains of the students sitting in Mr. Smith's classroom. The amygdala was probably active during this entire, far from novel, read-aloud activity. However, the emotional content of this science lesson on air pressure was more than likely negative, and the sticky note used by the amygdala more than likely flagged this as a negative attitude toward science. Not exactly the learning outcome Mr. Smith was looking for when he developed this lesson plan.

Let's walk across the hall to visit a second eighth-grade science classroom exploring the very same concept, air pressure. Students walk in to find a lab basket containing an Erlenmeyer flask, a measuring cup, an index card, graph paper, and a box of markers at each of their tables. Mrs. Smith (no relation to Mr. Smith) asks her students to look at the supplies in the lab basket with the other members of their group and to make predictions about what they are going to do with the supplies. After a brief time, she asks the students to use the materials in the lab basket to follow a simple set of procedures:

1. Select a person at your table to fill the measuring cup with water.

2. Fill the Erlenmeyer flask half-full with water.

3. Place the index card on top of the Erlenmeyer flask.

4. While using your hand to hold the card securely on the top of the flask, turn the flask over.

5. Remove your hand and record your observations.

The room is alive with *ohhhhhs* and *ahhhhhs* during this novel event. Some groups have trouble following directions and spill water everywhere. Mrs. Smith assures them that this is okay and encourages them to get a new index card and to try again until the card appears to hold the water in the flask. Or is it the card? After several minutes, Mrs. Smith stops the students and asks them to share their thoughts about the activity. Students provide incredible accounts of the activity, incorporating all of the spills and thrills from the water task.

Teacher: *Please take a few moments and record your observations in your science notebooks.*

The teacher walks around the room to spot-check the students' observations. Once she has noticed that they are all finished, she continues.

Teacher: *As you were working, I hung up four different signs around the room.*

Teacher identifies and points to each sign:

   Moisture convergence

   Air pressure

   Atmospheric stability

   Inversion

Teacher: *Individually make a prediction about why the card appeared to hold the water in the flask.*

   Please move to the sign that matches your prediction.

   Find a partner and share your thoughts about why you made this prediction.

Using pairs will increase the level of active participation.

Teacher: *Now return to your seats.*

   The activity we just completed is a demonstration of today's topic. Using your textbooks, see whether you and your group members can find the explanation for why the card appeared to hold the water in the flask.

From this point forward, Mrs. Smith continues her lesson on air pressure. The fundamental difference between these two classrooms lies in the use of novelty to elicit students' positive emotions while learning. As a result, these two classrooms will also differ in the quality of learning outcomes. The student brains in Mrs. Smith's class will experience positive emotions as a result of the opening activity. The emotional content of this science lesson on air pressure will more than likely be positive, the sticky note used by the amygdala will more than likely flag this as a positive feeling toward science, and the student is more likely to recall the content of the lesson. The two classrooms of Mr. and Mrs. Smith demonstrate the importance of novelty as a way to incorporate emotionally charged events into the classroom.

Emotionally Charged Events

In the science and the mathematics classroom, emotional charged events are referred to as "emotional hooks." There are several applications of this brain principle that come to mind. Hooking students up to a machine that emits a moderate electric shock into the palm of their hands every time they miss a multiplication fact, leave out a force on their free-body diagram, or forget the astronomical term for the inevitable fate of large, oversized stars would certainly make learning an emotionally charged event. However, this is not an advisable use of the brain's emotional networks. Instead, is there a way to tap into the positive emotions that help drive attention and memory? In other words, learning has to feel right, and if the learner feels good, he or she is more likely be engaged in your classroom (Jensen, 2005). In the end, emotions strongly influence our attention, help us make meaning of our experiences, and imprint strong memories in our brain (Berry et al., 2012; Chen & Williams, 2012; King & Williams, 2009; LeDoux, 1996; Miyashita & Williams, 2003; Schicknick et al., 2012; Whalley, 2012; Wolfe, 2010). Examples of emotional hooks include discrepant events, music, physical movement, game-like activities, and healthy competition. Let's start with discrepant events, and for this, we need to tap into the skills of Olympic figure skaters.

Lessons Learned From Olympic Figure Skating

Roller blades pose a significant challenge for many of us. Staying upright without grabbing hold of the first sturdy and stationary object is a virtual impossibility. Slipping on a pair of lace-up shoes with a thin metal blade attached the bottom of each shoe and then proceeding to move across a thin sheet of ice seems even more ludicrous. Even the most athletic person appreciates the performance of an Olympic figure skater. So what can the likes of Scott Hamilton, Brian Boitano, Dorothy Hamill, and Kristi Yamaguchi teach us about student engagement? Well, it has to do with a particular stunt that each of them is quite exceptional at performing. Let's explore the teaching strategy "discrepant events."

Nothing awakens the amygdala, cingulate gyrus, and PFC while at the same time getting the dopamine pumping like a surprise ending. If you did not see the end coming, or if you expected something totally different, your brain has an electrochemical eruption, leaving it craving an explanation for what happened and why that particular outcome happened. In science, we call these bizarre outcomes "discrepant events." What brings students to the edges of their seats is the "surprising, often counterintuitive outcome [that] creates cognitive disequilibrium that temporarily throws learners mentally off-balance" (O'Brien, 2010, p. xi). Discrepant events can take the form of a demonstration, a hands-on activity performed by the students, or a video clip from the Internet.

Let's return to our discussion of Olympic figure skaters. The day was Tuesday and the 19 Introductory Physics students compliantly shuffled into first period. The class began with several video clips of the most recent Olympic figure skating competition. Although there were some giggles and snickers at the idea of watching Olympic figure skating, there was also a unanimous crowd of puzzled faces. Here is how the rest of the introduction unfolded.

Teacher: *How many of you are a slight bit curious about what this video clip has to do with this physics class?*

Teacher waits as students raise their hands or look around in confusion.

Teacher: *I will give you a hint: There is a very strong connection between this video clip and today's physics class. Take a few moments and talk with a neighbor. See whether you and your neighbors can make some predictions about how Olympic figure skating relates to today's class. Go!*

Teacher pauses and lets the students make predictions with their neighbor.

Teacher: *Please pause where you are and say thank you to your neighbors for talking. Please share with me what you and your neighbors predicted.*

Teacher elicits student responses.

Teacher: *Could I please have a volunteer to come to the front of the room and sit on the spinning stool?*

Teacher waits for a student volunteer.

Teacher: *Please stick both of your arms straight out as if you are making the blades of a helicopter. While you are sitting on the stool, I am going to spin the stool around.*

Teacher spins the stool.

Teacher: *Now bring your arms in and give yourself a hug.*

If you are familiar with the demonstration, you will recall that the spinning student will pick up speed and spin around at a noticeably faster rate when his arms are brought close to his body. The students in your classroom will notice this as well and quickly *oh* and *ah* over this bizarre outcome. The very idea that bringing your arms in toward the center of your body causes you to spin at a noticeably faster rate is discrepant from what many of your students believe. Having your students discuss possible explanations for this phenomenon as well as linking this to the video clips of the Olympic figure skater are appropriate next steps. What is most important about this strategy is that the outcome or event is counterintuitive or contradictory to what the students believe, thus raising their level of engagement as their brains seek to make meaning of the discrepant event.

What about a mathematics classroom? Are there discrepant events for math? The answer is yes. For this example, you will need to recall your birthday. In a class of at least 23 people, there is a greater than 50% chance that two people share the same birthday. However, most students will refuse to believe this and take you, the teacher, up on any bet on this conjecture. As a math teacher, you want to take this bet and then use the outcome to help the students understand combinatorics (combinations), probability, and factorials. This discrepant event, often referred to as the Birthday Paradox, will be a novel introduction to and concrete experience with the three abstract ideas of combinations, probability, and factorials.

Stop-n-Think Box 4.3

Think about the essential learnings within your content area. What discrepant events could you add to the lesson as a way to add novelty and increase student engagement? Make a list.

Whether you show students that a playing card can hold against an inverted cylinder of water, a needle can go through a balloon without the balloon popping, that pure water does not conduct electricity, that infinite sequences and series converge to bizarre numbers, or that tapping the top of a vigorously shaken carbonated beverage can does not prevent it from spewing, a discrepant event can captivate, activate, and invigorate the brains of your science and math learners. And if you are curious and hung up on the shaken carbonated beverage, tap the sides of the vigorously shaken drink and see what happens. No spewing, but certainly an engaging way to discuss Boyle's Law and the law's potentially messy outcomes.

Using Music

As the saying goes, "If you can't beat 'em, join 'em." As our students meander through the hallways before and after school they are often tuned into their MP3 players for auditory stimulation. In many cases, students may ask whether they can listen to their MP3 players in class. Music does many different things for the brain, and this may be our students' way of telling us that they need this form of stimulation. So, can we use it in our classrooms? The answer is absolutely a yes!

Music can be used to further capitalize on novelty and provide an extremely successful emotional hook (Wolfe, 2010). Music is associated with positive cognitive, emotional, and behavioral outcomes that provide significant benefits to science and mathematics classrooms (Kelley & Berridge, 2002; Krumhansl, 1997; Menon & Levitin, 2005; Sloboda & Juslin, 2001). Cognitively, playing or listening to music appears to influence our visual-spatial, mathematical, and creative abilities (Levitin, 2006). Similarly, our endocrine systems, hormonal responses, social interactions, and personal skills are involved in playing or listening to music as well (Blood & Zatorre, 2001; Blood, Zatorre, Bermudez, & Evans, 1999). Music in the classroom is often a novel event that stimulates the RAS. Many music selections evoke a positive emotional response and thus trigger the amygdala to lace the experience with dopamine, placing a positive sticky note on the experience. And as an added bonus, music can be used for behavioral engagement to provide cues for what is happening or going to happen in the classroom. Imagine walking into a classroom each day where upbeat music is playing in the background. Hearing The Beach Boys, The Temptations, or The Four Seasons playing in the background before geometry class makes students take note that this is not your typical math class.

This class is novel. Music can be used four different ways in the science and mathematics classroom:

1. Music for beginning or starting the class

2. Music for ending or leaving class

3. Music for transitions

4. Music for working and thinking

The type of music that is appropriate depends on the way it is to be used and on the particular task that the music is to accompany. For example, if students are summarizing their understanding of Coulomb's Law or writing out a general procedure for solving quadratic equations, playing Marilyn Manson in the background is both counterproductive and inappropriate. As a result, there are five general rules for using music in the classroom:

1. Words should not compete with words. When students are writing or reading, the music should be instrumental.

2. If music agitates even a single student in the classroom, stop using it! No strategy is worth causing anxiety in a student.

3. Keep in mind that what you find musically satisfying may not align with what a 16-year-old listens to. Get caught up with the times or use '60s and '70s music.

4. Screen all music for appropriate language. In most cases, the "clean version" of a song can be purchased through online music sites.

5. Finally, never, ever let the students pick the music.

Music for Beginning Class

As the name suggests, music for beginning class is the music playing when students are entering the classroom. As science and mathematics teachers, we want our students to be as energized and excited as we are about our content areas. Thus, the selection of music should be upbeat, positive, and promote generally good feelings in the students shuffling into our classrooms. Sixties music is a great place to start and, believe it or not, crosses the generations in evoking positive responses in the brain. However, there are some great songs from the current generation of performers that work just as well.

Stop-n-Think Box 4.4

Here are some songs to use for beginning class.

"Good Vibrations" by The Beach Boys

"Happy Days" by Pratt and McClain

"Rockin' Robin" by Bobby Day or The Jackson 5

"Me and My Gang" by Rascal Flatts

"Crocodile Rock" by Elton John

"At the Hop" by Danny and the Juniors

"Great Balls of Fire" by Jerry Lee Lewis

"Shake Me, Wake Me" by The Four Tops

"I Got You (I Feel Good)" by James Brown

Now add more songs you might use for the beginning of class.

When you stop the song is certainly up to the individual teacher. However, the tardy bell serves as a natural stopping point, or you can stop it when you are ready to provide them with information. Simply stop the music and begin!

Music for Ending Class

This particular use of music is a blast and when used effectively, very funny for students. Once class is over, sending them away with positive emotions is just as important as starting the class period with positive emotions. This music serves as a cognitive and behavioral cue that says, "We are done for the day." In a very important way, it brings closure to the class period or day, keeping in mind that students' emotions leaving the class will influence the emotions they return with next time.

Stop-n-Think Box 4.5

Here are some songs to use for ending class.

"Happy Trails" by Dale Evans and Roy Rogers

"Hit the Road Jack" by Ray Charles

(Continued)

(Continued)

"What a Wonderful World" by Louis Armstrong

"Hallelujah Chorus" from Handel's *Messiah*

"See You Later Alligator" by Bill Haley and His Comets

"Pomp and Circumstance" by Elgar

Now add more songs you might use for the end of class.

Music for ending class keeps playing until the last student leaves. Now it is time to reset the MP3 player, CD player, or computer for the next class's beginning class music.

Music for Transitions

If there is even a brief pause in the action, teenagers will find a way to fill it. Behaviorally, transitions can be a challenge for classroom teachers because students view the redirection from one activity to the next as an opportunity to cut loose. Although not a cure-all, using music to fill moments of silence in the classroom is a tool for both behavioral and emotional engagement. The type of music most appropriate for transitions is music that is high in beats per minute and that also has a strong backbeat for "hurrying" things along. Songs like the *William Tell Overture* by Gioachino Rossini or the theme from *Mission Impossible* are emotionally and behaviorally arousing, often exciting students by the fact that they recognize the song and then spurring students to action.

When should these songs be used in the classroom? Ultimately, the choice will depend on the students in the classroom and the tolerance level of both the students and the teacher. An excellent place to start is anytime students are moving from one activity to the next and the teacher needs this to happen expeditiously. The following are two specific examples.

1. A math teacher opens class by asking, "Please get out your homework from last night and a writing utensil." He or she then plays "Start Me Up" by the Rolling Stones.

2. A science teacher instructs students, "Move into your laboratory groups to complete a pre-laboratory exercise." He or she then plays "I've Been Everywhere" by Johnny Cash.

Moving students from individual work to partner or small group work, to and from laboratory areas, or waiting for them to get out supplies or materials are all times that could use a little pick-me-up music.

Stop-n-Think Box 4.6

Here is a list of songs for transitions.

"Let's Get Loud" by Jennifer Lopez

"Rock This Town" by the Stray Cats

"Something to Talk About" by Bonnie Raitt

"9 to 5" by Dolly Parton

"25 Miles" by Edwin Starr

"Good Lovin'" by The Rascals

"(We're Gonna) Rock Around the Clock" by Bill Haley and His Comets

Now add more songs you might use for class transitions.

As teachers incorporate music into the classroom for transitions, the natural movement of the students from one activity to the next will become more efficient. What is most beneficial to teachers is that students will learn that starting the music means "go" and stopping the music means, well, "stop." Over time, when the music stops, students will pause and look in your direction in anticipation of the next set of instructions. Once students arrive at the next activity or task, can music facilitate the working and thinking process? The answer is yes.

Music for Working and Thinking

Using music for working and thinking is a bit more challenging than the three previous uses for classroom music. The reason has to do with the cognitive processing of information. First of all, when students are reading silently, don't play music! When students are reflecting or making meaning of content, music with high beats per minute or lyrics can be distracting and interfere with reflection and meaning making. However, if students are engaged in conversation, discussing or debriefing about content or information, music can help to focus the conversation on the partner or group discussion and away from other classroom distractions or other group conversations. As a general rule of thumb, when students are reflecting or making meaning of content (e.g., making a concept map, writing a reflection, or completing a guided practice problem) there should either be silence or soft classical or instrumental music. Examples of music that work in this situation include selections from *The Four Seasons* by Vivaldi, Brandenburg Concerto No. 2 by Bach, "Gagliarda" by Galilei, or the famous theme from *Forrest Gump* by The O'Neill Brothers. Other possible selections are instrumental selections that are commonly associated with spas and tranquility. Keep in mind that monitoring student reactions to music for reflecting will help to decide whether it is better to just maintain silence. This is a decision that only the classroom teacher can make, and it may vary from day to day.

When students are engaged in conversation, discussing or debriefing about content or information, the music should be upbeat and at a moderate volume. There are several reasons why music is helpful with classroom engagement in this situation. The most successful way to move something from short-term memory to long-term memory is to tell someone what you know (Medina, 2008). However, when teachers ask students to discuss something with a neighbor or group, we are met with awkward silence and stares from students. No student wants to be the first to start talking, nor does he or she want other classmates or the teacher to overhear what is being said. The fix to this situation is to play music during this time of conversation, discussion, and debriefing at a volume that prevents both of these awkward scenarios (i.e., being the first to talk and being overhead by neighbors or the teacher).

> The teacher has just finished working two examples of solving and graphing linear inequalities. She pauses and waits for the students to finish copying the worked examples into their notebooks. This is done in silence.
>
> Teacher: *Now, please turn to your neighbor and decide who will be "A" and who will be "B."*
>
> The teacher waits a few seconds for students to make this decision.
>
> Teacher: *If you are an "A," you will explain and summarize to your partner, "B," how to solve the first example. Then "B," you will do the same with the second example. You have about two-and-a-half minutes. Go!*
>
> The teacher plays the song "Blue Suede Shoes" by Carl Perkins.

A biology teacher has just finished presenting content focused on cellular respiration, specifically the Krebs cycle.

Teacher: *Please take a few minutes and, in your science notebooks, write down the information you need to know about the Krebs cycle, using the notes on the board as your guide. Go!*

This is done in silence.

The teacher waits a few minutes to provide time for students to fill in their notes.

Teacher: *Please get out your textbooks and find the section on cellular respiration.*

The teacher starts the song "Rhythm Nation" by Janet Jackson. Once the students have their books out, he pauses the music.

Teacher: *Take a few minutes and skim the section on the Krebs cycle. Please read it silently. When you are finished, look up.*

The teacher waits until the students have finished reading and given him the cue by looking up. This is done in silence.

Teacher: *With the information you have just read, please edit, add to, or adjust your notes. Take about a minute and a half to complete this task. Go.*

The teacher plays Sonata No. 3 by Mozart. After about a minute and a half, the teacher pauses the music.

Teacher: *Now, turn to your neighbor and take turns sharing your notes. Make changes as you see necessary. You have two minutes for this sharing. Go.*

The teacher plays the song "Love Train" by The O'Jays.

Although music for any of the purposes presented in this chapter may seem like a trivial strategy that is a waste of time, keep in mind the purpose of both this book and the recipe. To truly captivate, activate, and invigorate the student brain, teachers have to create an environment that is both enticing and inviting to students. What may seem trivial or minor to us as teachers may make a world of difference to the students and their perception of the classroom. Novelty through music does just that by making the classroom a place students want to enter. Once the students want to be in the classroom, what happens next is discussed in another chapter. Give music a try!

Movement With a Purpose

There is an urban legend about the inventor of the modern school desk (circa the late 1800s). An interesting feature of this story is that some argue that the inventor was a woman who did not get credit for the invention due to the social climate of the late 1800s. More to the point, someone asked him, or her, why the desks were made to be so uncomfortable. The response, if this urban legend is true, was quite shocking. The inventor's response strongly suggested that the desks did not need to be comfortable because students would only spend a brief amount of time in the desks. The majority of the time would be spent out of their seats exploring and learning. Do you believe his or her vision of school and learning is accurate?

Our bodies and brains like to move. Students who move have brains that groove. Physical movement provides several brain benefits that work together to promote engagement and facilitate the learning process: increased blood flow, oxygen levels, and glucose utilization; increased levels of dopamine and norepinephrine; and increased growth of new brain cells (Almarode & Almarode, 2008; Colcombe & Kramer, 2003; Colcombe et al., 2004; Hillman, Erickson, & Kramer, 2008; Kramer, Colcombe, McAuley, Scalf, & Erickson, 2005; Medina, 2008; Olson, Eadie, Ernst, & Christie, 2006; Ratey & Hagerman 2008).

More specifically, physical activity increases the production of the brain-derived neurotrophic factor, or BDNF. This particular growth factor acts like fertilizer for brain development in the hippocampus, the cerebral cortex, and the basal forebrain. Each of these areas is vital for learning, memory, and higher-order thinking (Colcombe et al., 2006; Colcombe & Kramer, 2003; Cotman & Berchtold, 2002). Other physiological changes include angiogenesis, the growth of new blood vessels; neurogenesis, the growth of new brain cells; and synaptogenesis, the formation of new brain connections (Brown et al., 2003; Ratey & Hagerman, 2008).

The importance of dopamine was discussed earlier in the chapter and is involved in emotionally charged events and creating sticky notes for the brain. However, this is the first time we have mentioned norepinephrine. Norepinephrine is a catecholamine that functions both as a hormone and as a neurotransmitter (Ratey & Hagerman, 2008). Relevant to this discussion, norepinephrine is released when an event or stimulus is deemed risky, urgent, or exciting (Jensen, 2003). The release of norepinephrine is like super glue for memories; it helps lock memories into place (Ratey & Hagerman, 2008). Because movement in the classroom is often a novel event for students, movement is also exciting and triggers the release of the memory super glue, norepinephrine.

The take-home message here is that movement is an example of novelty that activates the reticular activating system and a host of other physiological responses that jumpstart student engagement. However, movement without a purpose can be chaotic and turn raucous. Purposeful movement in the science and mathematics classroom is commonly referred to as *energizers* (Almarode & Almarode, 2008). Energizers are brief, movement-based activities that are placed throughout a lesson or class period. These energizers should incorporate purposeful movement rather than "free time." Although this purposeful movement does not have to incorporate academic content (e.g., stretch breaks or bathroom breaks), lacing an energizer with content results in cognitive arousal and the review or exploration of content, a two-for-one special. Let's look at some examples.

Movement With a Purpose 1: A New Perspective

To review content or material from the previous class period, have students relocate to have a discussion with classmates who are not their immediate neighbors. Have students stand up, grab their notes, and find a new place to sit in the classroom. Make sure they are sitting with someone who is not their immediate neighbor. Using music while they find their new seat can increase the energy in the room as well. Once they are in new seats, have students review their notes with one or two of their new neighbors. You can add more structure to this activity by providing a list of review questions that the student groups are responsible for answering. New content can also be taught while students are in the new seat and while their brains are still energized from the novelty. After students return to their original seat, have them review with a neighbor what they learned while they were "away."

Movement With a Purpose 2: Answer With Your Feet

Make each wall of the classroom an answer to a multiple-choice question by placing a giant "A" on one wall, "B" on a second wall, and so on. Present the class with a multiple-choice question. After allowing them to read and think of a response, have students stand, chat with their classmates, and move to the area of the room that matches their response to the question. A variation of this energizer is to put specific concepts on the walls. For example, when studying cell reproduction, make each wall a different stage of mitosis. Place a written description or visual of a specific stage of mitosis on the screen or board. Students must then move to the region of the room that has the correct answer. This can also be done with other science topics, such as the geologic time scale, Newton's laws of motion, or types of chemical reactions.

Movement With a Purpose 3: Snowball Fight

A snowball fight can be used to review material or activate prior knowledge. Students develop one or two questions about class topics on a sheet of paper and place their names somewhere on the sheet of paper. This can be done as a "bell ringer" or simply as a way to break up the class period after a segment of instruction. Students take their sheet of paper and ball it up into a "snowball." Have the students stand up and evenly divide themselves into two groups, standing on opposite sides of the room. After balling the questions up into "snowballs," each side throws them across the room to their peers. Each student answers the questions on his or her newly acquired "snowball," either by writing a response directly on the paper or finding the author of the questions and discussion the responses.

Stop-n-Think Box 4.7

How do you ask your students to exchange information and thoughts? Think about the activities or strategies you use that are done while students are sitting still. Be creative and embed some action. Use the following chart to brainstorm ideas for getting students "out of their seat and on their feet."

Strategies	Strategies in Action
Example: Exchange papers with your neighbor.	Concentric Circles (Inside/Outside Circle)
Example: "Turn to" your neighbor and share your thoughts about . . .	Stand Up–Hand Up–Pair Up

---

Movement With a Purpose 4: You Are Not Going to Want to Miss This

For really important concepts, have students stand up and gather closely around the board or projection screen. After explaining the key point, have them summarize the information to someone standing close to them. This is also a great way to emphasize certain topics without the traditional rhetoric of telling students to remember it because it will be "on the test," and it provides students a new perspective on the content.

Goldilocks and the Three Bears: Novelty in Moderation

When it comes to making decisions, biology, economics, psychology, astrobiology, and many other academic disciplines call upon "Goldilocks and the Three Bears" for wisdom. Believe it or not, this way of thinking is referred to as the Goldilocks paradigm. Although not a proven scientific fact, the Goldilocks paradigm suggests that desired outcomes arise from making sure the conditions follow the same rules as Goldilocks and her porridge: not too hot, not too cold, but just right. In the area of child development and the nature versus nurture debate, the same thinking applies. To produce the desired outcome, a happy and healthy child, the environment should be just right. Teachers should look at novelty and this part of the recipe through the same lens. Too much novelty will cause chaos. Too little novelty and the classroom will be nothing but routine and lack the required stimulation of the RAS, amygdala, cingulate gyrus, and PFC that the brain needs. The amount of novelty needs to be just right.

What is just right depends on a host of factors, not the least of which is the students in the classroom. This chapter cannot provide a teacher with what is just right. In fact, no author, chapter, or book can answer that question. Instead, knowing what novelty does for the brain and building a toolkit of strategies for sprinkling a classroom with novelty is the best start to finding "just right." From there, each classroom teacher has to season and adjust to taste based on his or her unique classroom environment.

CHAPTER 4: EXIT TICKET

Based on the material presented in the chapter, fill in the following graphic organizer. Give careful consideration to how this information is relevant to your classroom and student learning.

Photo from Thinkstock.com.

Part of the Brain	This part is like . . .	Draw the Analogy	Relevance to the Classroom
Reticular activating system	venetian blinds		
Amygdala			
Cingulate gyrus			
Prefrontal cortex			

Engaging Professional Development Tasks

1. This professional development task encourages you to reflect upon an upcoming lesson plan and locate places where you could embed discrepant events and novelty. First, find a lesson plan that you have previously taught. Look over the lesson plan and reflect on the use of discrepant events and novelty. Begin by reflecting on the level of student engagement:

   - What was engaging about the lesson? Was it physical (movement) or was it designed around mental (critical or creative thinking) engagement? What type of active participation was utilized (overt and/or covert)?
   - What parts of the lesson were not particularly engaging?

Now spend a few minutes examining the lesson for evidence of discrepant events and other forms of novelty:

   - Did you offer students a novel experience or discrepant event within this lesson?
   - Design a discrepant event that would offer a pick-me-up in student engagement.

Now use this reflective practice to guide the planning of an upcoming lesson:

   - Where can you provide a discrepant event to add novelty and promote engagement?
   - What factors should you consider in selecting that discrepant event?

Try out this lesson and reflect upon how it worked or did not work. What did you notice about student engagement?

2. This professional development task encourages you to experiment with the use of music and movement in your classroom. Just like the previous professional development task, locate a lesson plan from earlier in the year, one you have already taught. Look over the lesson plan and reflect on the potential use of music and movement. Then ask yourself the following questions:

- How much downtime or awkward silence occurred during the lesson?
- Where in the lesson plan could I have used music?
- How long were students required to sit during the lesson?
- Where in the lesson could I have used movement or gotten my students out of their seats?

Now use this reflective practice to guide the planning of an upcoming lesson:

- Where can you use music and movement to add novelty and promote engagement?
- What factors should you consider in selecting music and movement?

Try this out and reflect upon how it worked or did not work. What did you notice about student engagement?

References

Almarode, J., & Almarode, D. (2008). Energizing students. Maximizing student attention and engagement in the science classroom. *The Science Teacher, 75*, 32–35.

Banilower, E. R., Smith, P. S., Weiss, I. R., & Pasley, J. D. (2006). The status of K–12 science teaching in the United States. Results from a national observation study. In D. W. Sunal & E. L. Wright (Eds.), *The impact of state and national standards on K–12 science teaching* (pp. 83–149). Charlotte, NC: Information Age.

Berry, J. A., Cervantes-Sandoval, I., Nicholas, E. P., & Davis, R. L. (2012). Dopamine is required for learning and forgetting in drosophila. *Neuron, 74*(3), 530–542.

Blakemore, S. J. (2008). The social brain in adolescence. *Nature Reviews Neuroscience, 9*, 267–277.

Blakemore, S. J. (2012). Imaging brain development: The adolescent brain. *NeuroImage, 61*(2), 397–406.

Blakemore, S. J., & Choudhury, S. (2006). Development of the adolescent brain: Implications for executive function and social cognition. *Journal of Child Psychology and Psychiatry, 47*(3–4), 296–312.

Blood, A. J., & Zatorre, R. J. (2001). Intensely pleasurable responses to music correlate with activity in brain regions implicated in reward and emotion. *Proceedings of the National Academy of Sciences, U.S.A., 98*(20), 11818–11823.

Blood, A. J., Zatorre, R. J., Bermudez, P., & Evans, A. C. (1999). Emotional responses to pleasant and unpleasant music correlate with activity in paralimbic brain regions. *Nature Neuroscience, 2*(4), 382–387.

Braver, T. S., Reynolds, J. R., & Donaldson, D. I. (2003). Neural mechanisms of transient and sustained cognitive control during task-switching. *Neuron, 39,* 713–726.

Breiter, H., Etcoff, N. L., Whalen, P. J., Kennedy, W. A., Rauch, S., Buckner, R. L., . . . Rosen, B. R. (1996). Response and habituation of the human amygdala during visual processing of facial expression. *Neuron, 17,* 875–887.

Brown, J., Copper-Kuhn, C. M., Kempermann, G., Van Praag, H., Winkler, J., Gage, F. H., & Kuhn, H. G. (2003). Enriched environment and physical activity stimulate hippocampal but not olfactory bulb neurogenesis. *European Journal of Neuroscience, 17,* 2042–2046.

Cahill, L., Babinsky, R., Markowitsch, H. J., & McGaugh, J. L. (1995). The amygdala and emotional memory. *Nature, 377*(6547), 295–296.

Cahill, L., & McGaugh, J. L. (1995). A novel demonstration of enhanced memory associated with emotional arousal. *Consciousness and Cognition, 4*(4), 410–421.

Cahill, L., & McGaugh, J. L. (1998). Mechanisms of emotional arousal and lasting declarative memory. *Trends in Neurosciences, 21*(7), 294–299.

Chen, C. C., & Williams, C. L. (2012). Interactions between epinephrine, ascending vagal fibers and central noradrenergic systems in modulating memory for emotionally arousing events. *Frontiers in Behavioral Neuroscience, 6*(35), 1–20.

Choudhury, S. (2010). Culturing the adolescent brain: What can neuroscience learn from anthropology? *Social Cognitive Affective Neuroscience, 5*(2–3), 159–167.

Colcombe, S. J., Erickson, K. I., Scalf, P. E., Kim, J. S., Prakash, R., McAuley, E., . . . Kramer, A. F. (2006). Aerobic exercise training increases brain volume in aging humans. *Journal of Gerontology: Medical Sciences, 61A*(11), 1166–1170.

Colcombe, S., & Kramer, A. F. (2003). Fitness effects on the cognitive function of older adults: A meta-analytic study. *Psychological Science, 14*(2), 125–130.

Colcombe, S. J., Kramer, A. F., Erickson, K. I., Scalf, P., McAuley, E., Cohen, N. J., . . . Elavsky, S. (2004). Cardiovascular fitness, cortical plasticity, and aging. *Proceedings of the National Academy of Sciences, U.S.A., 101*(9), 3316–3321.

Cotman, C. W., & Berchtold, N. C. (2002). Exercise: A behavioral intervention to enhance brain health and plasticity. *Trends in Neuroscience, 25*(6), 295–301.

Crawford, G. B. (2007). *Brain-based teaching with adolescent learning in mind* (2nd ed.). Thousand Oaks, CA: Corwin.

Dolcos, F., LaBar, K. S., & Cabeza, R. (2004). Interaction between the amygdala and the medial temporal lobe memory system predicts better memory for emotional events. *Neuron, 42,* 855–863.

Feinstein, S. G. (2009). *Secrets of the teenage brain: Research-based strategies for reaching and teaching today's adolescents* (2nd ed.). Thousand Oaks, CA: Corwin.

Friedenberg, J. D., & Silverman, G. (2012). *Cognitive science: An introduction to the study of the mind* (2nd ed.). Thousand Oaks, CA: Sage.

Gonen, T., Admon, R., Podlipsky, I., & Hendler, T. (2012). From animal model to human brain networking: Dynamic causal modeling of motivational systems. *Journal of Neuroscience, 32*(21), 7218–7224.

Harmon-Jones, E., & van Honk, J. (2012). Introduction to a special issue on the neuroscience of motivation and emotion. *Motivation and Emotion, 36*, 1–3.

Hennenlotter, A., Schroeder, U., Erhard, P., Castrop, F., Haslinger, B., Stoecker, D., . . . Ceballos-Baumann, A. O. (2005). A common neural basis for receptive and expressive communication of pleasant facial affect. *NeuroImage, 26*(2), 581–591.

Hillman, C. H., Erickson, K. I., & Kramer, A. F. (2008). Be smart, exercise your heart: Exercise effects on brain and cognition. *Nature Reviews Neuroscience, 9*, 58–65.

Jensen, E. (2003). *Tools for engagement: Managing emotional states for learner success.* San Diego, CA: The Brain Store.

Jensen, E. (2005). *Teaching with the brain in mind* (2nd ed.). Alexandria, VA: Association for Supervision and Curriculum Development.

Kelley, A. E., & Berridge, K. C. (2002). The neuroscience of natural rewards: Relevance to addictive drugs. *Journal of Neuroscience, 22*(9), 3306–3311.

King, S. O. II, & Williams, C. L. (2009). Novelty-induced arousal enhances memory for classical fear conditioning: Interactions between peripheral adrenergic and brainstem glutamatergic systems. *Learning and Memory, 16*, 625–634.

Kramer, A. F., Colcombe, S. J., McAuley, E., Scalf, P. E., & Erickson, K. I. (2005). Fitness, aging and neurocognitive function. *Neurobiology of Aging, 26*(S), S124–S127.

Krumhansl, C. L. (1997). An exploratory study of musical emotions and psychophysiology. *Canadian Journal of Experimental Psychology, 51*(4), 336–353.

LeDoux, J. (1996). *The emotional brain: The mysterious underpinnings of emotional life.* New York: Touchstone.

LeDoux, J. (2002). *Synaptic self: How our brains become who we are.* New York: Viking Press.

Levitin, D. J. (2006). *This is your brain on music: The science of a human obsession.* New York: Penguin.

Lindquist, K. A., Wager, T. D., Kober, H., Bliss-Moreau, E., & Barrett, L. F. (2012). The brain basis of emotion: A meta-analytic review. *Behavioral and Brain Sciences, 35*, 121–202.

McGaugh, J. L. (2004). The amygdala modulates the consolidation of memories of emotionally arousing experiences. *Annual Reviews of Neuroscience, 27*, 1–28.

Medina, J. (2008). *Brain rules. 12 principles for surviving and thriving at work, home, and school.* Seattle, WA: Pear Press.

Menon, V., & Levitin, D. J. (2005). The rewards of music listening: Response and physiological connectivity of the mesolimbic system. *NeuroImage, 28*(1), 175–184.

Miyashita, T., & Williams, C. L. (2003). Enhancement of noradrenergic neurotransmission in the nucleus of the solitary tract modulates memory storage processes. *Brain Research, 987,* 164–175.

Nieoullon, A., & Coquerel, A. (2003). Dopamine: A key regulator to adapt action, emotion, motivation and cognition. *Current Opinions in Neurology, 2*(S), 3–9.

O'Brien, T. (2010). *Brain-powered science: Teaching and learning with discrepant events.* Alexandria, VA: National Science Teachers Association.

Olson, A. K., Eadie, B. D., Ernst, C., & Christie, B. R. (2006). Environmental enrichment and voluntary exercise massively increase neurogenesis in the adult hippocampus via dissociable pathways. *Hippocampus, 16,* 250–260.

Posner, M. I., & Dehaene, S. (1994). Attentional networks. *Trends in Neuroscience, 17*(2), 75–79.

Posner, M. I., & Peterson, S. E. (1990). The attention system of the human brain. *Annual Reviews of Neuroscience, 13,* 25–42.

Ratey, J. J., & Hagerman, E. (2008). *Spark. The revolutionary new science of exercise and the brain.* New York: Little, Brown and Company.

Raz, A., & Buhle, J. (2006). Typologies of attentional networks. *Nature Reviews Neuroscience, 7,* 367–379.

Ripke, S., Hubner, T., Mennigen, E., Muller, K. U., Rodehacke, S., Schmidt, D., . . . Smolka, M. N. (in press). Reward processing and intertemporal decision making in adults and adolescents: The role of impulsivity and decision consistency. *Brain Research.*

Schicknick, H., Reichenbach, N., Smalla, K. H., Scheich, H., Gundelfinger, E. D., & Tischmeyer, W. (2012). Dopamine modulates memory consolidation of discrimination learning in the auditory cortex. *European Journal of Neuroscience, 35*(5), 763–774.

Shirey, L. L. (1992). Importance, interest and selective attention. In K. A. Renninger, S. Hidi, & A. Krapp (Eds.), *The role of interest in learning and development* (pp. 281–296). Hillsdale, NJ: Lawrence Erlbaum.

Sloboda, J. A., & Juslin, P. (2001). Psychological perspectives on music and emotion. In P. Juslin & J. A. Sloboda (Eds.), *Music and emotion: Theory and research* (pp. 71–104). Oxford, UK: Oxford University Press.

Somerville, L. H., Kim, H., Johnstone, T., Alexander, A. L., & Whalen, P. J. (2004). Human amygdala responses during presentation of happy and neutral faces: Correlations with state anxiety. *Biological Psychiatry, 55*(9), 897–903.

Whalley, K. (2012). Learning and memory: Becoming a habit: A role for NMDA receptors. *Nature Reviews Neuroscience, 13,* 72.

Willis, J. (2006). *Research-based strategies to ignite student learning. Insights from a neurologist and classroom teacher.* Alexandria, VA: Association of Supervision and Curriculum Development.

Wolfe, P. (2010). *Brain matters: Translating research into classroom practice* (2nd ed.). Alexandria, VA: Association for Supervision and Curriculum Development.

5

Why Do We Need to Know This?

Establishing Relevance

Stop-n-Think Box 5.1

A student in your class has just asked, "Do we have to know this for the test?" What is your response? How do you respond to students who bluntly ask, "Why do we need to know this?"

This part of the recipe is all about relevance and how the brain craves a response to the infamous question, "Why do we need to know this?" Just as people will eat if they are hungry and the food in front of them is appetizing, the brain is more likely to engage with content if it is hungry for the content and finds the topic appetizing. Unfortunately, making a room full of adolescents hungry for solubility rules, Gauss's Law, logarithmic functions, or the simplifying of rational expressions is not a trivial task. Let's face it, directly linking many of the concepts in our science and mathematics classrooms to the daily lives of our students is not realistic. Plus, we cannot fake this attempt at relevance because our students are on to us and will likely disengage at the very idea that we think they would fall for such an attempt.

Ultimately, a meaningful relationship must be formed between the learner and the information being presented in the science and mathematics classroom. When teachers make conscious decisions to form relevant and credible connections between the students' lives and the information being learned, teachers are actually increasing the probability that students will retain that knowledge. Not only can these relevant and credible connections increase retention, but relevance also has the potential to increase the rate and degree of learning, stimulate motivation, and promote transfer (Frymier & Shulman, 1995; Keller, 1983, 1987; Newby, 1991; Sass, 1989). What teacher does not want these outcomes for her students? The fine print is that relevance does not just happen. Adolescents are notorious for their underdeveloped skills in long-range planning. Establishing relevance takes deliberate planning and intentional implementation in the classroom. Establishing relevance requires teachers to anticipate questions like "Do we have to know this for the test?" and "Why do we need to know this?" The appetite of our teenage learners for science and mathematics must often be explicitly guided, nudged, and influenced.

Stop-n-Think Box 5.2

How do you establish meaningful relationships between your course's content and the students in your classroom? List some specific examples.

Inside the walls of a geometry class in a local high school, a young ninth grader sits and watches intently as his teacher explains a right triangle trigonometry problem. Once the teacher selects the appropriate trigonometric ratio (i.e., sine, cosine, or tangent), the young student raises his hand to ask the teacher a question that he believes is a good one. "Mrs. Smith, when will we ever use this in real life?" Without hesitation, Mrs. Smith enters into a monologue about building a wooden swing set for her daughter. As the story goes, she needed to use trigonometry and the relationships between the angles and sides of a triangle to determine how far apart to place the support beams of the wooden swing set. The male author of this book was the young ninth grader in this story, and the geometry teacher's response did not work! For one thing, a ninth grader is not likely to find the construction of a swing set relevant to him or her while sitting in a geometry class. Second, when you put swing sets together for your children, grandchildren, nieces, nephews, or any other child, did you use trigonometry? Not likely!

So what do we do with this situation? Can we make science and mathematics learning relevant to our teenage students without faking it? The answer is, as you have come to expect, a definite yes. Establishing relevance begins with a small, furry, powder-white, four-legged creature; the part of his brain known as the *nucleus basalis;* and a necessary brain chemical called *acetylcholine.*

How Is Relevance Good for the Brain? A Mouse Tale

Melvin and his many rodent relatives occupy cages in research laboratories across the world and participate in a variety of research studies that are invaluable to humans. The particular experiment relevant to this chapter involves a swimming pool with a transparent podium called a Morris Water Tank (see Figure 5.1). A Morris Water Tank is often used to study the memory formation, learning, and problem-solving abilities in mice (e.g., Miyoshi et al., 2012). Results of such studies provide valuable insight into human memory, learning, and problem solving.

The Morris Water Tank experiment provides a fascinating look at the role of relevance in the brain and learning. It relies on the fact that

Figure 5.1   Morris Water Tank

mice hate to swim. Hidden below the surface of the water is a transparent podium that, when discovered by the mouse, provides the little four-legged research assistant with a place to stand with only his or her little feet in the water. This is the ideal location for the frantic mouse that is quickly trying to find his or her way out of the water. Once on the podium, the mouse is rewarded by being dried off and then returned to the cage with a treat.

So what is the point of all of this mumbo-jumbo about a mouse? First, the location of the podium is behaviorally relevant to the mouse. That is, learning the location of the podium sparks an internal response in the brain that provides clear and acceptable answers to the mouse asking, "Why do I need to know this?" The answer is that learning the location of the podium gets the mouse out of the water. When neuroscientists look at the brain of a mouse that has not only participated in the Morris Water Tank task but mastered the location of the podium, a specific area of the brain is highly active: the nucleus basalis (see Figure 5.2; Butt et al., 2009; Kilgard & Merzenich, 1998).

Figure 5.2   Nucleus Basalis

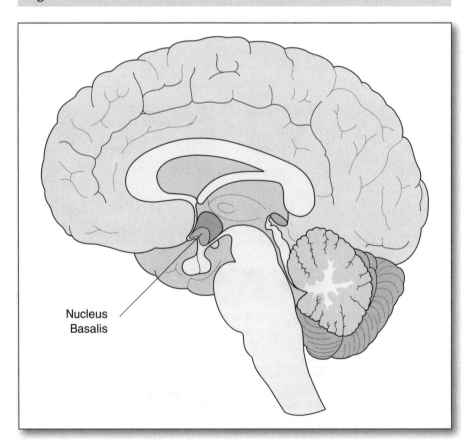

Nucleus
Basalis

The nucleus basalis is a collection of neurons in the middle of the brain that becomes very active when something is judged to be behaviorally relevant (e.g., finding the location of the podium to get out of the water; Chiba, Bucci, Holland, & Gallagher, 1995; Kilgard & Merzenich, 1998; McGaughy, Dalley, Morrison, Everitt, & Robbins, 2002; Sarter, Bruno, & Givens, 2003; Waite, Wardlow, & Power, 1999). When the nucleus basalis is activated, this collection of neurons triggers the release of an abundance of acetylcholine (Kilgard & Merzenich, 1998; Mesulam, Mufson, Wainer, & Levey, 1983; Phillis, 1968; Rasmusson, 2000). Acetylcholine is a neurotransmitter that is absolutely essential in the formation of the types of memories we rely on in the science and mathematics classroom (Klinkenberg, Sambeth, & Blokland, 2011; Rasmusson, 2000). That's right; when something is deemed to be behaviorally relevant, a neurophysiological chain of events is set into motion that actually increases the formation of memories associated with the behaviorally relevant event (Butt & Bowman, 2002; Butt & Hodge, 1997; Butt, Noble, Rogers, & Rea, 2002; Cabrera, Chavez, Corley, Kitto, & Butt, 2006; De Bartolo et al., 2008; Kilgard & Merzenich, 1998).

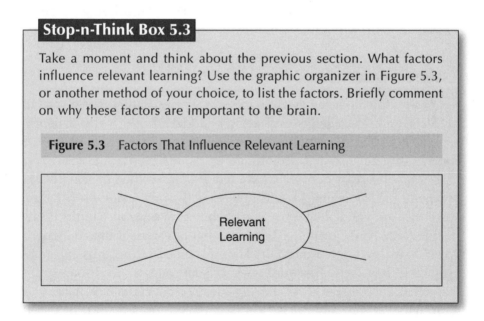

Stop-n-Think Box 5.3

Take a moment and think about the previous section. What factors influence relevant learning? Use the graphic organizer in Figure 5.3, or another method of your choice, to list the factors. Briefly comment on why these factors are important to the brain.

Figure 5.3   Factors That Influence Relevant Learning

Relevant
Learning

The most valuable insight from this research is the distinction between life relevance and behavioral relevance (Frymier & Houser, 1998; Kelly & Gorham, 1988). In the scenario described at the beginning of this chapter, Mrs. Smith was trying to create life relevance. In other words, Mrs. Smith was hoping that her students would deem the content in the science and mathematics classroom relevant to their lives now and in their future. Our brain, however, is happy with something being behaviorally relevant and worthy of its immediate attention (Frymier & Houser, 1998; Kelly & Gorham, 1988). That is, the brain is simply looking for stimuli or experiences that make it say, "Sure, I will play along, participate, and engage in what you have to offer."

Stop-n-Think Box 5.4

Before we examine this idea any further, compare and contrast life relevance and behavioral relevance. Can you think of a time when you used life relevance in your classroom? How successful were you? Now do the same for behavioral relevance. Which technique seems easier for you?

How Can I Make Learning Behaviorally Relevant?

There are several ways to make learning behaviorally relevant: (1) essential questions, (2) engaging scenarios, (3) offering students choices, and (4) game-like activities and inconsequential competition.

Essential Questions

Questioning strategies were introduced in Chapter 3 as a way to activate prior knowledge and get the student brain ready to learn. Open versus closed questions and questions that elicit, probe, or extend student thinking provide an engaging avenue for activating prior knowledge by digging up student understanding of science and mathematics concepts. In addition to activating prior knowledge, questions are valuable in providing behavioral relevance in the classroom. Larry Ainsworth (2003) argues that questions pose challenges to students, invite them into the learning process, and thus are more engaging than facts. Essential questions are one or two broad questions that encompass all of the key ideas or concepts in a particular unit, while at the same time "lead students to understand for themselves what their teachers want them to learn" (p. 45; see Table 5.1).

The creation and use of essential questions in science and mathematics provides a framework for all other ideas and concepts in a given unit while framing each individual lesson taught in that unit. In other words, essential questions help teachers answer the question, "Why do I need to know this?" or "What does this have to do with

Table 5.1   Examples of Essential Questions

Science	Mathematics
Unit on scientific notation: What is scientific notation? What is the benefit of using scientific notation over standard notation?	Unit on derivatives: How do we find the slope of a graph that is not linear? What information does this provide for us?
Unit on cell physiology: What are the basic building blocks of our body, and how do they work together?	Unit on variables: What is a variable, and why is it necessary in mathematics?
Unit on geology: Where do rocks come from, and what do they tell us about Earth?	Unit on triangle trigonometry: What is the relationship between the sides and the angles of a triangle? How do these relationships differ from other polygons?
Unit on nuclear reactions: What does it mean for an atom to be unstable? What makes an atom stable?	Unit on quadratics: Why does a quadratic equation have two solutions?

anything?" The answer to essential questions is the collective list of big ideas or concepts associated with the unit. Wiggins and McTighe (2005) define essential questions as "questions that are not answerable with finality in a brief sentence. . . . Their aim is to stimulate thought, to provoke inquiry, and to spark more questions—including thoughtful student questions—not just pat answers" (p. 106). In order to think in terms of questions, "instead of thinking of content as something to be covered, consider knowledge and skill as the means of addressing questions central to understanding key issues in your subject" (p. 107).

Powerful essential questions have several characteristics in common: (1) they are broad and incorporate the ideas, concepts, and topics of a particular unit; (2) they help students make sense of the information by providing a guiding framework for the content; (3) the "correct" answer to an essential question requires the use of all ideas, concepts, and topics within the framework; and (4) they encourage students to make connections between individual ideas, concepts, and topics in a unit (Ainsworth, 2003; Wiggins & McTighe, 2005).

So how does a teacher develop essential questions? The answer lies within the standards or curriculum for a particular class (e.g., Algebra 1, Earth Science, Calculus, or Physics). To develop questions that will engage the learner's mind and assist each student in answering the question, "Why do I need to know this?" familiarity with the specific state or national standard is paramount. Let's work through the process of developing essential questions in Stop-n-Think Box 5.5.

Stop-n-Think Box 5.5

First, read through the steps in the process. Then examine the two examples we have provided and create an essential question for your classroom.

1. Select a specific state or national standard for a specific science or mathematics class that you currently teach. Write down that standard, including all subsections and essential skills it contains.

2. In a standard there are important nouns that represent the ideas, concepts, or topics students must master. Nouns are the building blocks of essential questions. Make a list of the important nouns in the standard you selected.

3. Write one or two sentences that summarize what the nouns have in common.

4. Finally, turn this summary into one or two questions.

Example 1: Science

Topic: The Rock Cycle

1. Earth Science Standard 6 (Virginia Standards of Learning): The student will investigate and understand the rock cycle as it relates to the origin and transformation of rock types and how to identify common rock types based on mineral composition and textures. Key concepts include
   (a) igneous rocks;
   (b) sedimentary rocks; and
   (c) metamorphic rocks.

2. Important Nouns: rock cycle, origin, transformation, rock types, mineral composition, textures.

3. Summary Statement: The rock cycle is a geological process that describes the transformation over time of three rock types. This

dynamic process creates a variety of rocks through changes in environmental forces.

4. Essential Questions: Where do rocks come from? What do they tell us about the Earth?

Example 2: Geometry

Topic: Triangles

1. Geometry Standard 5 (Virginia Standards of Learning): The student, given information concerning the lengths of sides and/or measures of angles in triangles, will

   (a) order the sides by length, given the angle measures;
   (b) order the angles by degree measure, given the side lengths;
   (c) determine whether a triangle exists; and
   (d) determine the range in which the length of the third side must lie.

These concepts will be considered in the context of real-world situations.

2. Important Nouns: length, sides, measures, angles, order, degree, triangle, range.

3. Summary Statement: For triangles, there is a fundamental relationship between the length of the sides and the measure of the angles.

4. Essential Questions: What is the relationship between the sides and the angles of a triangle? How do these relationships differ from other polygons?

Now it is time for you to follow the steps and establish an essential question for one of your units of study. Go!

Once you have identified your essential questions for a particular unit, display them in the room on a large poster, and refer to them each day by asking students to relate that day's learning to the essential questions. Explicitly link the day's objectives to the essential questions, and use these connections to check for understanding, generate exit activities, or form questions for a final assessment. Students may not see the life relevance of the rock cycle or the measurements of angles within a triangle, but essential questions help make the learning behaviorally relevant by providing a framework and sense-making opportunity for these adolescent learners. Don't be surprised if your essential questions stimulate students to ask you questions. This is a good thing, and it is called engagement!

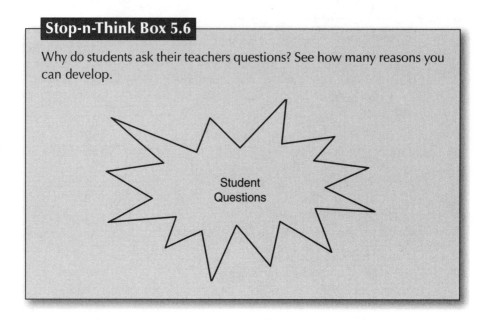

When responding to Stop-n-Think Box 5.6, did you find yourself writing words and ideas like "feeling confused," "dissatisfaction with information being presented," "curious to know something," or "wants a better explanation"? How about words like "skepticism," "discrepancy," or maybe even "a feeling of disequilibrium"? What is your typical response when you discover a student who is feeling confused or skeptical or dissatisfied? Most teachers respond with reassurance. This could appear in the form of a prompt toward the correct response or additional information that will clear up the confusion. Teachers do whatever they can to reduce these types of feelings in their students. Did you know that essential questions are designed to stimulate curiosity, a feeling of wonder, and a strong desire to ask questions? Essential question stimulate the need for relevance, which stimulates and encourages students to think more critically, ask more questions, and become more actively involved in the learning process (Ainsworth, 2003; Wiggins & McTighe, 2005).

Engaging Scenarios

As we continue our discussion about essential questions, let's discuss how to create an engaging scenario in our classrooms. Engaging scenarios make learning behaviorally relevant by providing a meaning-making experience that enables students to assimilate new learning into an authentic context or framework (Wolfe, 2010). Teaching any science or mathematics concept as abstract, independent, or isolated information makes it very difficult for the brain to attach meaning and to find the content behaviorally relevant. For example, teaching nuclear reactions in physics or chemistry as a series of equations and rules for the emission of an alpha, beta, or gamma particle focuses on an abstract process that has very little meaning to the average teenage science student. Students cannot see, hear, or relate to a helium nucleus jumping out of a uranium-238 nucleus, magically transforming the atom into thorium-234. Similarly, presenting quadratic equations as a series of algorithms about how to solve for the set of solutions (i.e., graphing, completing the square, factoring, or the quadratic formula) offers very little meaning to the average teenage math student. Nuclear reaction and quadratic equations are abstract ideas to teenage students, and their brains would prefer to learn about them with a concrete, meaning-making experience. The brain rule is that we learn from concrete to abstract (Willingham, 2009; Wolfe, 2010). One idea that provides a concrete, meaning-making experience for the student brain is the use of an engaging scenario.

An engaging scenario provides an authentic context that then creates an engaging learning experience for students (Ainsworth, 2010). Engaging scenarios are teacher-created stories presented at the beginning of a unit of study that motivate students by providing (1) an authentic context for the science and mathematics learning; (2) a job or role for the student to play in this context; (3) an audience to which this scenario is targeted; and (4) a collection of performance tasks (no more than five) that must be completed by the student (McTighe & Brown, 2005). Let's look at two examples of an engaging scenario.

Engaging Scenario 1

Physics or Chemistry: Nuclear Reactions

You are world-renowned nuclear scientist who works for a university in the same city in which you live. One evening, your local six o'clock news announces that the United States has decided to increase the nuclear infrastructure to reduce the country's level of carbon emissions. As a result, your city has been selected by the Department of Energy as the next location for a nuclear power plant. As you are well aware, there is significant debate about the use of nuclear energy, and it is sure to be contentious among your neighbors and fellow citizens.

The mayor of your city calls you in desperate need of some advice and your expertise. You are being asked to serve as a consultant to the

(Continued)

(Continued)

city council and help them decide whether to fight this decision to build a nuclear power plant or embrace the selection of your city. You must develop a presentation to inform the public and city officials and deliver it at a public hearing. How can you get ready for this very important presentation and ensure that you provide unbiased, well-supported information to your fellow citizens?

Performance Task 1: Use Cornell notes to gather information on nuclear reactions.

Performance Task 2: Compare and contrast nuclear reactions with other types of reactions in chemistry or physics.

Performance Task 3: Design or create a model or drawing that illustrates the function of a nuclear power plant.

Performance Task 4: Develop a comprehensive list of the pros and cons of nuclear energy compared with other forms of energy production.

Performance Task 5: Develop a 20-minute presentation making a case for or against the use of nuclear energy.

Notice that the engaging preceding scenario included an authentic story line, an authentic role for the student, an audience for fulfilling this role, and a series of performance tasks. Teachers can then develop rubrics or guidelines for the successful completion of the performance tasks.

Stop-n-Think Box 5.7

Take a moment and identify the parts of Engaging Scenario 1. Circle, underline, or highlight the authentic context or storyline, the role of the student, the audience, and the performance tasks.

Engaging Scenario 2

Advanced Algebra: Quadratic Equations

You are an exceptionally talented mathematician who also happens to be a movie buff. You have been contacted by *Mythbusters* to help them bust a movie myth wide open . . . or validate that the stunt is possible. In the 1994 action-adventure film *Speed*, the bad guy equipped a Los

Angeles bus with a bomb that was set explode if the speed of the bus fell below 50 mph (22 m/s). The police discovered the bomb and routed the bus on to a segment of freeway that was still under construction—their intention being to keep it out of the notoriously heavy Southern California traffic. In a twist of the plot, however, they overlooked a 50-foot (15 m) gap in the construction. Because the bomb would explode, killing everyone on board, if they slowed down, they decided to jump the gap at a speed of 67 mph (30 m/s).

The producers and hosts of *Mythbusters* need your help! You will provide the mathematical calculations for this episode and present them in a way that the television audience will understand. How will you go about doing this?

Performance Task 1: Compare and contrast quadratic equations with linear equations.

Performance Task 2: Create a graph of a quadratic equation that illustrates the essential features of the function.

Performance Task 3: Select two examples of a quadratic equation and find their solutions. Create a study aid for other students by recording yourself solving the two quadratic equations.

Performance Task 4: Prepare a video segment of you busting or validating the Los Angeles city bus scene from the movie *Speed*.

When engaging scenarios are placed at the beginning of a unit of study, these authentic contexts enable students to make meaning from concrete experiences and spark behavioral relevance in the science and mathematics content. Although these scenarios are ideal for the beginning of the unit, they can be easily adapted to jump-start engagement in the middle of a unit or as a way to close a unit of study.

Stop-n-Think Box 5.8

Develop a list of units for the science and mathematics classes that you teach. Select one unit of study from the list and develop and engaging scenario for that unit.

Unit of Study: _____

Situation: _____

(Continued)

(Continued)

Role of the Student: _____

Audience: _____

Performance Tasks:

1.

2.

3.

4.

Now write the narrative for this engaging scenario.

Student Choice

Have you ever seen a buffet-style restaurant with an empty parking lot on a Sunday afternoon? More than likely, the answer to this question is no. A buffet-style restaurant is an obvious choice for a large group because it offers the greatest likelihood that everyone in the dining party will find something palatable. The science and mathematics classroom works the same way, only choice in this situation refers to assignments and not food. A second strategy for creating behavioral relevance in the classroom is to provide students with choices for tasks and assignments. By providing a buffet, albeit a small buffet, of options, you make your students feel more empowered, and they are more likely to take ownership of the task or assignment. Giving students choices not only creates ownership, it is known to increase motivation and student engagement. Student choice offers options for differentiations at almost every phase of the learning process (Gregory & Chapman, 2008; Gregory & Hammerman, 2008; Tomlinson, 1999, 2001). Student choice is appropriate for in-class assignments as well as homework or out-of-school projects.

In-Class Choice

Students can be given choices about how they want to take notes, reflect on their learning, or process the content. For example, there is a wide range of methods for taking notes (e.g., Cornell notes or two-column notes; see Figure 5.4).

Figure 5.4 Examples of Two-Column Cornell Notes

Cornell Two-Column Notes

keywords:	Notes:
	Types of Matter
Solids	I. Solids
	A. Hold a particular size and shape
	B. Have a specific volume
Liquids	II. Liquids
	A. Do not have a shape
	B. Have size or volume
Gases	III. Gases
	A. Do not have color or shape
	B. Do not have volume

Summary:
(Insert summary of lecture after class)

Chapter 12: Waves Transfer Energy

A wave is a disturbance - transfers energy - Started by a force - moves through a medium	- When a slinky is stretched, the individual coils assume an equilibrium or rest position
	- When the first coil of the slinky is repeatedly vibrated back and forth, a disturbance is created which travels through the slinky from one end to another
Types of waves - Transverse - Longitudinal	
	- Slinky waves can be made by vibrating the first coil back and forth in either a horizontal or vertical direction

(Continued)

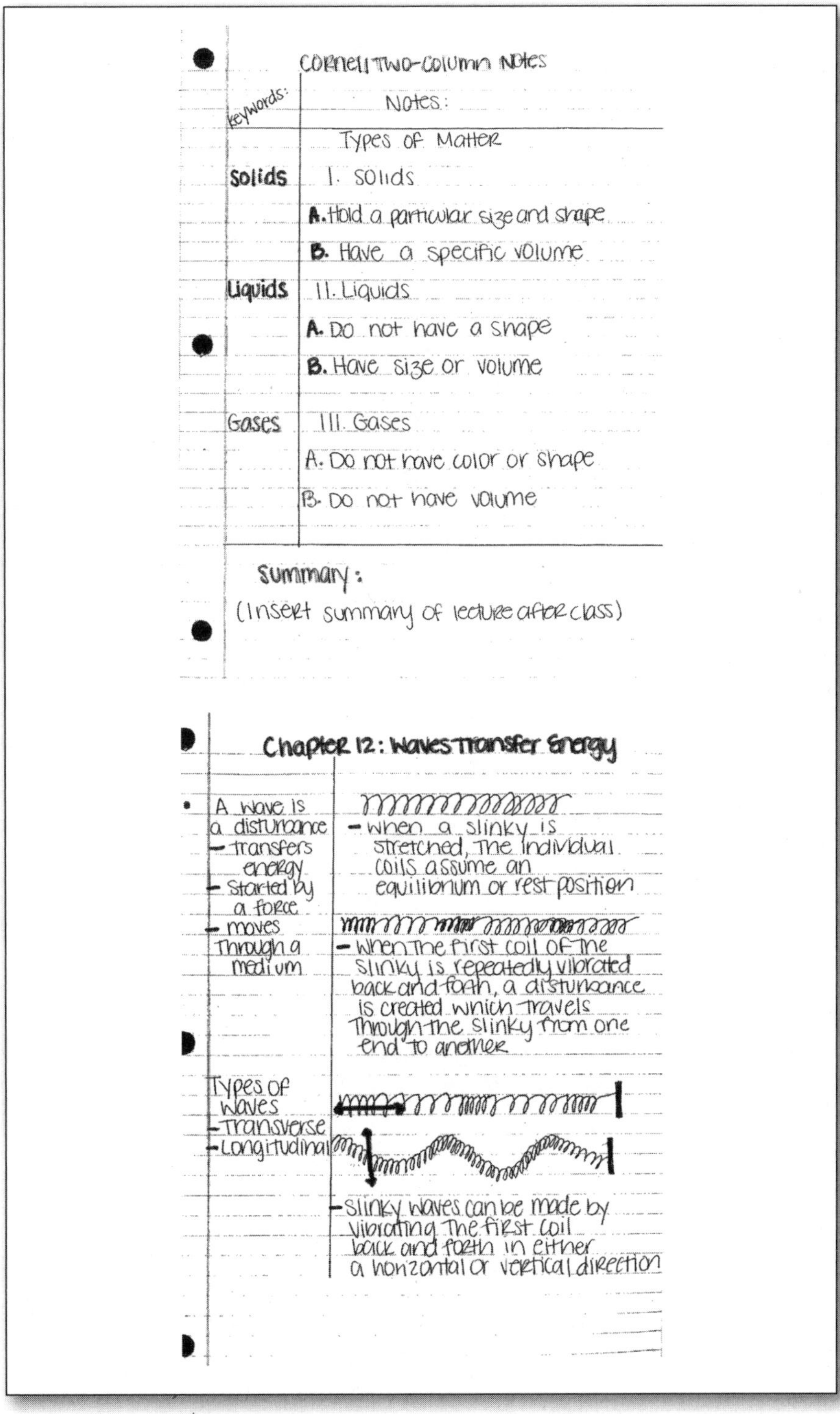

Figure 5.4 (Continued)

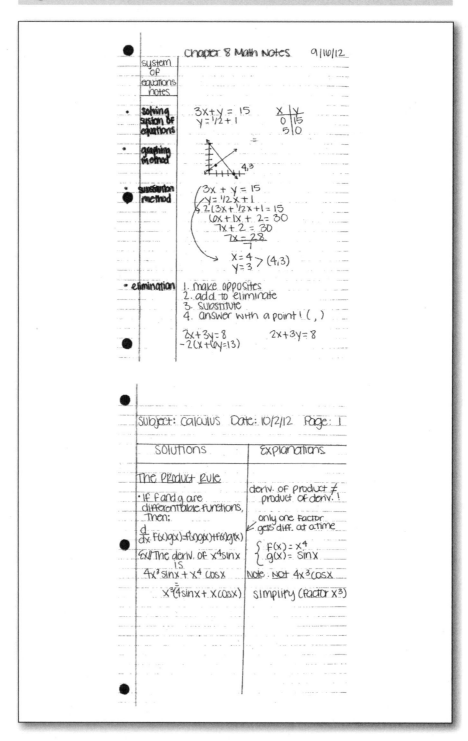

Source: Julianna Sproul. Used with permission.

> ### Stop-n-Think Box 5.9
>
> How do your students take notes? What are other styles or formats for student note taking? Create a list of note-taking strategies that you will model for your students.

Note taking is addressed in greater detail in a later chapter; in this chapter, we wish to emphasize the importance of modeling note-taking strategies for your students. Once students have experienced Cornell notes, two-column notes, or any of the strategies you listed in Stop-n-Think Box 5.9, let them choose a method for a particular lesson or class period. As a follow-up, have students turn to their neighbors and share the method of note taking they selected, review the content of their notes, and reflect on why it was or was not an effective method for this particular content.

A similar approach can be taken when students are asked to reflect upon their learning or process content. After a learning segment on the states of matter, systems of equations, mechanical waves, or the product rule, offer students a variety of options for processing or reflecting upon their learning.

Here are several examples for reflecting or processing student learning:

1. Using your notes, write a brief one- or two-sentence summary.

2. Create a concept map from your notes.

3. Draw a picture of . . .

4. Think about how you would explain this to someone who has not taken this class.

5. Take turns reviewing your notes with a neighbor or partner.

6. Develop two or three questions about this material that you would like to see on the next quiz or test.

7. Use sticky notes and extract two or three key ideas or concepts from your notes.

8. What are two or three things you are not 100% clear about?

What other choices can you think of? Add to the list.

Creating a list of options and posting them in a conspicuous location in the classroom enables the teacher to pause and ask students to select a task from the list and complete it. Once students have completed a reading assignment, observed a demonstration, or completed a lesson on any science or mathematics topic, provide them with a list of choices to further develop their understanding.

Homework Choice

Students truly appreciate choice when completing homework assignments. Try sending home a choice board (Gregory & Chapman, 2008; Gregory & Hammerman, 2008). Table 5.2 is an example of a choice board on proportional reasoning.

As the teacher distributes the choice board to each student, clear directions must be given: "Complete one option in each row. Check the box of the choice you made and turn the choice board in with your solutions."

Table 5.2   Proportional Reasoning Choice Board

☐ Design several ways for solving proportional problems. You might use a pict-o-gram, poem, or flow chart.	☐ Identify ways to recognize a proportional situation? How do you explain proportionality?	☐ As you try to solve a proportional problem, what do you think about? Write a list of questions that you could ask yourself as you try to solve a proportional problem.
☐ Where do you find proportional reasoning in the world today. Using this information construct a word problem that requires proportional reasoning. Explain why it required proportional reasoning.	☐ With a partner, design a list of sequential steps to use for solving a proportional problem.	☐ Do you use proportional reasoning in your life? If so; explain why it is proportional and how you utilize it.
☐ Generate a story that utilizes a proportional situation. Be prepared to demonstrate and explain your story to the class.	☐ Use your text book to locate and solve a word problem that requires proportional reasoning. In your math journal explain how you solved the problem.	☐ Where do you see proportional situations? Create a list of proportional situations in the world today. Share your list with a partner.

If you examine Table 5.2 carefully, you will discover that the options are grouped in columns according to varying levels of difficulty. The middle column contains the lower-level questions, the tasks in the third column are within the average range, and the tasks in the first column are a bit more challenging. As teachers observe the student choices and examine their individual responses, they will gain insight into the depth of student knowledge about proportional reasoning. Students will feel empowered by the fact that they only have three problems to complete for their homework, instead of all nine. Choice boards are an excellent way to differentiate instruction in all content areas. There are a variety of ways to construct these boards that will address individual readiness levels, learning styles, and student interests. An ideal starting place for compiling such a list is Bloom's Taxonomy. This will ensure that the options you are offering to your students include different levels of rigor as well as a variety of thinking levels.

In the late 1950s, a group of educational psychologists headed by Benjamin Bloom developed a classification system of cognitive behaviors valuable for learning and called it Bloom's Taxonomy (Anderson & Sosniak, 1994; Bloom, Englehart, Furst, Hill, & Krathwohl, 1956; Krathwohl, 2002; Marzano, 2001). The cognitive levels span from the most basic of tasks, like regurgitating information, to the most complex cognitive activities, such as evaluating information or content with a critical eye (see Table 5.3).

The particular level of Bloom's Taxonomy on which the student is working depends on the student's level of understanding

Table 5.3 Bloom's Original Taxonomy

1. Knowledge: The student recalls or remembers information.

2. Comprehension: The student explains ideas and concepts.

3. Application: The student uses information in a different way.

4. Analysis: The student deconstructs the knowledge into different components and determines how the components relate to one another and the overall concept.

5. Synthesis: The student brings together various ideas and components and develops a comprehensive product or performance task.

6. Evaluation: The student uses the ideas and concepts to critically evaluate or take a stand for a particular viewpoint.

and the amount of rigor designed by the science or mathematics teacher. In other words, students can move from level to level within the same unit, lesson, or class period. In fact, students should have the opportunity to work at all levels of Bloom's Taxonomy to ensure they are developing a deep understanding of the content.

In the early 1990s, a group of cognitive psychologists, instructional researchers, and testing and assessment specialists evaluated (ironically, the highest level of cognitive behaviors in the original Bloom's Taxonomy) the original Bloom's Taxonomy and revised it to reflect the most recent work in educational and cognitive psychology. As a result of their work, these cognitive psychologists, headed by Lorin Anderson, one of Bloom's students, changed the top level of cognitive behaviors from evaluating to creating (Anderson & Sosniak, 1994; Krathwohl, 2002). In the end, they "created" the revised Bloom's Taxonomy (see Table 5.4).

Probably the most helpful feature of "Bloom's Taxonomy 2.0" is the list of verbs and nouns associated with each level of cognitive behavior. These verbs and nouns make the translation of Bloom's Taxonomy into classroom activities almost seamless. With regard to student choice, all teachers need to do is design a buffet of activities derived from the various levels of Bloom's Taxonomy. Once students have completed a reading assignment, observed a demonstration, or completed a lesson on any science or mathematics topic, they simply pick an activity to further develop their level of understanding. The most important thing to remember about this list is to include all levels of the taxonomy. As students move toward understanding, the choices they are offered should incorporate higher levels of Bloom's Taxonomy. Student choice paired with cognitively complex tasks makes for more relevant learning (Marzano, Pickering, & Heflebower, 2010).

Game-Like Activities and Inconsequential Competition

Just like watching the person sitting next to you at the dinner table take the last homemade biscuit, losing out on something is not fun. Yet, games make any activity, and the associated content, behaviorally relevant. This makes for a delicate balance in the science and mathematics classroom. How do we create a game-like activity that promotes behavioral relevance without having someone lose and subsequently disengage? The answer: Create game-like activities for partners or small groups.

Table 5.4   Bloom's Revised Taxonomy

Level		Verbs and nouns associated with the level
1. **Remembering**	Can the student recall or remember information?	define, duplicate, list, memorize, recall, repeat, reproduce, state
2. **Understanding**	Can the student explain ideas or concepts?	classify, describe, discuss, explain, identify, locate, recognize, report, select, translate, summarize
3. **Applying**	Can the student use the information in a different way?	demonstrate, illustrate, use, write, interpret, dramatize
4. **Analyzing**	Can the student distinguish between the different components of ideas or concepts?	appraise, compare, contrast, criticize, differentiate, discriminate, distinguish, examine, experiment, question, test
5. **Evaluating**	Can the student justify an opinion or viewpoint with the ideas or concepts?	argue, defend, judge, select, support, value, evaluate
6. **Creating**	Can the student create a new product?	assemble, construct, create, design, develop, formulate, write

Source: Adapted from Anderson and Sosniak (1994).

Taboo

Take the classic party game and add a slight twist to make it a behaviorally relevant, game-like activity. Taboo is a team game in which one member of the team draws a card that has a pop-culture word at the top. The goal of the person drawing the card is to get his or her teammates to guess the word. However, there is a catch. On the card, just below the featured word, is a list of words that cannot be used as clues. As you can probably imagine, the words on the "do not say" list are the first ones that come to mind when describing the featured word. This leads to creative fun for everyone.

In the classroom, this game works the same way, with one minor change. Instead of a list of words that cannot be said, students have to guess the main word *and* the associated words on the list (see Figure 5.5).

Figure 5.5   Vocabulary Game Examples

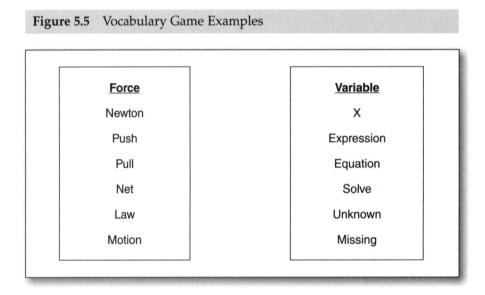

Force	**Variable**
Newton	X
Push	Expression
Pull	Equation
Net	Solve
Law	Unknown
Motion	Missing

For the two examples in Figure 5.5, partner students up. One partner will be the "talker" and the other will be the "guesser." The "guesser" must figure out the featured word (i.e., *force* or *variable*) along with all of the words below the featured word.

The secret in this strategy lies in the fact that students have to talk through concepts in such a way that makes them clear to their partners. To accomplish this behavioral task, students must cognitively formulate a deep understanding of the concepts to effectively and efficiently articulate the ideas to their partners. If teachers select abstract concepts like force and variable, students are required to construct concrete explanations, a natural progression in concept development (Willingham, 2009). In addition, in a room full of pairs guessing and laughing in a game-like activity, no one will know who guessed the words and who did not. That is inconsequential competition.

Stop-n-Think Box 5.10

Develop a list of key vocabulary and words associated with each term. Create a stack of Taboo cards to be used in your class.

$100,000 Pyramid

This popular game show from more than three decades ago provides a game-like activity for promoting behavioral relevance and conceptual understanding. As a brief refresher of the ins and outs of this game show, lets take a trip back to the 1980s. Partners accumulated money by guessing words associated with categories on a pyramid, like "things found in a kitchen." With Dick Clark at the helm, the big prize for the winning couple was $100,000.

The translation of this game show to the science and mathematics classroom is almost seamless. Using a template of the $100,000 Pyramid, picking the categories or key ideas to go in the spaces is a natural fit (see Figure 5.6 and Table 5.5). The teacher can decide whether to assign point values to the various locations on the pyramid.

Figure 5.6 $100,000 Pyramid

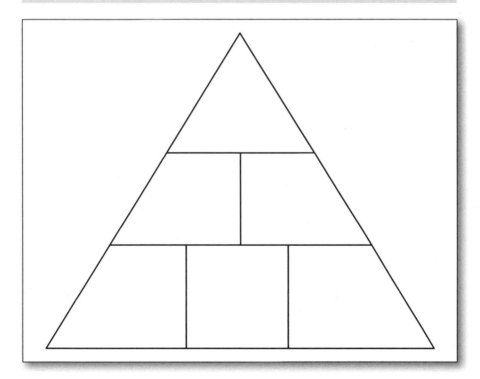

Table 5.5 Examples of Categories or Concepts for the Pyramid

Science	Mathematics
Simple machines	Steps to solving an equation
Types of rocks	Polygons
Types of chemical reactions	Trig identities
Parts of a cell	Statistical tests
Nonrenewable resources	Applications of a derivative
Laws of motion	Types of functions

Much like the variation on the game Taboo, this activity is an excellent way for partners to review concepts.

Stop-n-Think Box 5.11

The Internet is an excellent resource for game-like activities. Using your favorite search engine, download templates for games like the $100,000 Pyramid, Jeopardy, and Who Wants to Be a Millionaire? Construct one of these games based on current content in your course. How can you use these templates to foster behavioral relevance while at the same time creating inconsequential competition?

Link to the Recipe for Engagement

Students will often perceive information to be relevant if they find it is valuable, meaningful, purposeful, or useful. The activities just presented are examples of strategies for adding value, meaning, purpose, and utility that are also behaviorally relevant to the students. However, just like the thermostat on a convection oven, this value, meaning, purpose, or utility can be set at varying degrees for different students. Content that has significant relevance for one student may have little relevance for another student. With this in mind, teachers should design and engage students in learning experiences in which the relevance is transparent and exists along a continuum.

Take, for example, the landfall of Hurricane Rita. Hurricane Rita was the fourth-most intense Atlantic hurricane ever recorded. It came ashore on September 24, 2005, and Beaumont, Texas was one of the hardest-hit communities. For some, this event may have no relevance or meaning at all outside of the fact that they may have read about it in the newspapers or watched the media coverage from the comfort of their dry and still-standing house. For others, the meaning and relevance is quite high. On the very day that Hurricane Rita made landfall, a young woman, nine months pregnant, was faced with the fact that the local hospital was closed. After a 1,000-mile journey, this young woman arrived at a safe and dry home in a suburb of Richmond, Virginia, just in time to give birth to a beautiful baby girl. In the end, this nail-biting event made for a proud grandmother, who also happens to be one of the authors of this book. The point of this story is to highlight the idea that there are a wide range of personal interests, values, and real-world connections for every scenario or situation. This range of relevant connections will happen with almost any content in the science and mathematics classroom.

CHAPTER 5: EXIT TICKET

Think of several topics or learning segments within your content area. List several ways you can make the information relevant for your students. Following you will find a few continuum lines for turning up relevancy. Use this information to guide your thinking.

Photo from
Thinkstock.com.

Low personal significance	• • • • •	High personal significance
Does not relate to personal interests	• • • • •	Closely linked to personal interests
Little emotional implication	• • • • •	Strong emotional implication
No clear link to prior knowledge	• • • • •	Direct link to prior knowledge
No frame of reference for learner	• • • • •	Creates frame of reference for learner
No associations are constructed	• • • • •	Concrete associations are constructed
Unclear application in real world	• • • • •	Clear application in real world
No personal value for future use	• • • • •	High personal value for future use

Engaging Professional Development Tasks

1. This professional development task expands on the analogy of a thermostat and thermometer to decisions in the classroom. First, use Figure 5.7 to compare and contrast a thermostat and a thermometer.

Figure 5.7   Thermostat and Thermometer

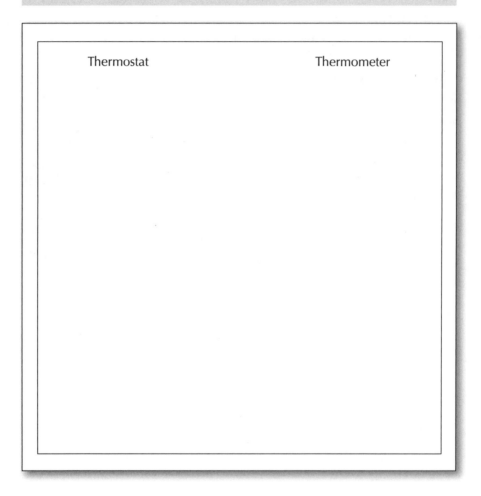

Thermostat   Thermometer

Thermometers are used to measure the temperature in a given environment. Put differently, thermometers react to the environment based on the thermal energy of the solid, liquid, or gas. On the other hand, a thermostat is a thermal energy regulator that is controlled or set to a desired temperature. How do these two objects resemble a science or mathematics classroom? Reflect on the nature of your teaching and the instruction decisions that go into each day. Sit down with a colleague and share this analogy with him or her. Use the following questions to guide your reflection and discussion:

- As you make instructional decisions in your classroom, are you a thermometer or a thermostat?
- Each day as you walk into your classroom, do you find yourself being reactive? Is your plan determined by your students' actions or the "temperature" of the learning environment? Or do you arrive ready to take action, initiate student learning, and anticipate questions, with a complete plan for implementation?
- What do you think this means?

Thermostats have a desired outcome. As you embed relevance into your classroom, be a proactive thermostat, regulating the amount and intensity of your connections, especially as you embed relevant connections for your students.

2. This professional development task encourages collaboration with colleagues to further develop and apply one of the strategies presented in this chapter. Set a time to collaborate with a colleague. Together, select one of the strategies presented in this chapter (e.g., essential questions, engaging scenarios, student choice, or game-like activities and inconsequential competition) and develop it for use. Each of you should try the strategy in an upcoming class. Afterward, set a debriefing time to reflect on the strategy of choice. Use the following questions to guide your reflection and discussion:

- How did you feel about the strategy?
- What did your students think about the strategy?
- Were you students more engaged?
- What evidence would support your answer?
- What would you do differently the next time?
- What are the next steps?

References

Ainsworth, L. (2003). *Unwrapping the standards: A simple process to make standards manageable.* Englewood, CO: Lead + Learn Press.

Ainsworth, L. (2010). *Rigorous curriculum design: How to create curricular units of study that align standards, instruction, and assessment.* Englewood, CO: Lead + Learn Press.

Anderson, L. W., & Sosniak, L. A. (Eds.). (1994). *Bloom's taxonomy: A forty-year perspective.* Chicago: University of Chicago Press.

Bloom, B. S., Englehart, M. B., Furst, E. J., Hill, W. H., & Krathwohl, O. R. (1956). *Taxonomy of educational objectives: The classification of education goals. Handbook 1: The cognitive domain.* New York: Longman.

Butt, A. E., & Bowman, T. D. (2002). Transverse patterning reveals a dissociation of simple and configural association learning abilities in rats with 192 IgG-saporin lesions of the nucleus basalis magnocellularis. *Neurobiology of Learning and Memory, 77,* 211–233.

Butt, A. E., Chavez, C. M., Flesher, M. M., Kinney-Hurd, B. L., Araujo, G. C., Miasnikov, A. A., & Weinberger, N. M. (2009). Association learning-dependent increases in acetylcholine release in the rat auditory cortex during auditory classical conditioning. *Neurobiology of Learning and Memory, 92,* 400–409.

Butt, A. E., & Hodge, G. K. (1997). Simple and configural association learning in rats with bilateral quisqualic acid lesions of the nucleus basalis magnocellularis. *Behavioral Brain Research, 89,* 71–85.

Butt, A. E., Noble, M., Rogers, J. L., & Rea, T. E. (2002). Impairments in negative patterning, but not simple discrimination learning, in rats with 192 IgG-Saporin lesions of the nucleus basalis magnocellularis. *Behavioral Neuroscience, 116,* 241–255.

Cabrera, S., Chavez, C., Corley, S., Kitto, M., & Butt, A. E. (2006). Selective lesions of the nucleus basalis magnocellularis impair cognitive flexibility. *Behavioral Neuroscience, 120,* 298–306.

Chiba, A. A., Bucci, D. J., Holland, P. C., & Gallagher, M. (1995). Basal forebrain cholinergic lesions disrupt increments but not decrements in conditioned stimulus processing. *The Journal of Neuroscience, 15,* 7315–7322.

De Bartolo, P., Leggio, M. G., Mandolesi, L., Foti, F., Gelfo, F., Ferlazzo, F., & Petrosini, L. (2008). Environmental enrichment mitigates the effects of basal forebrain lesions on cognitive flexibility. *Neuroscience, 154,* 444–453.

Frymier, A. B., & Houser, M. L. (1998). Does making content relevant make a difference in learning? *Communication Research Reports, 15*(2), 121–129.

Frymier, A. B., & Shulman, G. M. (1995). What's in it for me? Increasing content relevance to enhance students' motivation. *Communication Education, 44,* 40–50.

Gregory, G., & Chapman, C. (2008). *Differentiated instructional strategies. One size doesn't fit all* (2nd ed.). Thousand Oaks, CA: Corwin.

Gregory, G., & Hammerman, E. (2008). *Differentiated instructional strategies for science grades K-8.* Thousand Oaks, CA: Corwin.

Keller, J. M. (1983). Motivational design of instruction. In C. M. Reigeluth (Ed.), *Instructional design theories: An overview of their current status* (pp. 383–434). Hillsdale, NJ: Lawrence Erlbaum.

Keller, J. M. (1987). Strategies for stimulating motivation to learn. *Performance and Instruction, 26*(8), 1–7.

Kelley, D. H., & Gorham, J. (1988). Effects of immediacy on recall of information. *Communication Education, 37,* 198–207.

Kilgard, M. P., & Merzenich, M. M. (1998). Cortical map reorganization enabled by nucleus basalis activity. *Science, 279,* 1714–1718.

Klinkenberg, I., Sambeth, A., & Blokland, A. (2011). Acetylcholine and attention. *Behavioural Brain Research, 221*, 430–442.

Krathwohl, D. R. (2002). A revision of bloom's taxonomy: An overview. *Theory Into Practice, 41*(4), 212–218.

Marzano, R. J. (2001). *Designing a new taxonomy of educational objectives.* Thousand Oaks, CA: Corwin.

Marzano, R. J., Pickering, D. J., & Heflebower, T. (2010). *The highly engaged classroom.* Bloomington, IN: Solution Tree Press.

McGaughy, J., Dalley, J. W., Morrison, C. H., Everitt, B. J., & Robbins, T. W. (2002). Selective behavioral and neurochemical effects of cholinergic lesions produced by intrabasalis infusions of 192 IgG-saporin on attentional performance in a five-choice serial reaction time task. *The Journal of Neuroscience, 22*, 1905–1913.

McTighe, J., & Brown, J. L. (2005). Differentiated instruction and educational standards: Is détente possible? *Theory Into Practice, 44*(3), 234–244

Miyoshi, E., Wietzikoski, E. C., Bortolanza, M., Boschen, S. L., Canteras, N. S., Izquierdo, I., & Cunha, C. D. (2012). Both the dorsal hippocampus and the dorsolateral striatum are needed for rate navigation in the Morris water maze. *Behavioural Brain Research, 226*(1), 171–178.

Newby, T. J. (1991). Classroom motivation: Strategies for first-year teachers. *Journal of Educational Psychology, 83*, 181–195.

Phillis, J. W. (1968). Acetylcholine release from the cerebral cortex: Its role in cortical arousal. *Brain Research, 7*, 378–389.

Rasmusson, D. D. (2000). The role of acetylcholine in cortical synaptic plasticity. *Behavioural Brain Research, 115*, 205–218.

Sarter, M. F., Bruno, J. P., & Givens, B. (2003). Attentional functions of cortical cholinergic inputs: What does it mean for learning and memory? *Neurobiology of Learning and Memory, 80*, 245–256.

Sass, E. J. (1989). Motivation in the college classroom: What students tell us. *Teaching of Psychology, 16*(2), 86–88.

Tomlinson, C. A. (1999). *The differentiated classroom: Responding to the needs of all learners.* Alexandria, VA: Association for Supervision and Curriculum Development.

Tomlinson, C. A. (2001). *How to differentiate instruction in mixed-ability classrooms* (2nd ed.). Alexandria, VA: Association for Supervision and Curriculum Development.

Waite, J. J., Wardlow, M. L., & Power, A. E. (1999). Deficit in selective and divided attention associated with cholinergic basal forebrain immunotoxic lesion produced by 192 Saporin; Motoric/sensory deficit associated with Purkinje cell immunotoxin lesion produced by 0X7-Saporin. *Neurobiology of Learning and Memory, 71*, 325–352.

Wiggins, G., & McTighe, J. (2005). *Understanding by design* (2nd ed.). Alexandria, VA: Association for Supervision and Curriculum Development.

Willingham, D. T. (2009). *Why don't students like school? A cognitive scientist answers questions about how the mind works and what it means for the classroom.* San Francisco: Jossey-Bass.

Wolfe, P. (2010). *Brain matters. Translating research into classroom practice* (2nd ed.). Alexandria, VA: Association for Supervision and Curriculum Development.

6

Too Much, Too Fast

Maintaining an Engaging Pace

Why would someone leave beef, chicken, or pork to soak in a marinade before throwing the slab of meat on the grill or in the oven? Clearly, the resident chef is working to make the slab of meat both tasty and easier to chew.

Much like unmarinated meat, complex content in a science or mathematics classroom can lack flavor and be quite difficult to chew and swallow. Therefore, complex content should be covered with flavorful experiences that make the science and mathematics ideas, concepts, or topics more emotionally, behaviorally, and cognitively appealing, while at the same time making the content easier to mentally swallow and digest. At the same time, the adolescent brain can be immersed in complex learning and only take in so much information before it needs a break. The reason for this lies in the fact that the adolescent brain (and your brain) has input limitations (Baddeley, 1999; Cowan, 2001; Ericcson & Kintsch, 1995; Miller, 1956). Marinating the brain too long makes content very difficult to cognitively swallow and digest.

Input and Quantity Limitations

The adolescent brain can focus for about 10 to 12 minutes, on three to four chunks of information, before it needs a break (Baddeley, 1999;

Cowan, 2001). This is a natural and very reliable feature of the human brain. As Eric Jensen (2005) says, "too much, too fast, it won't last." Brain scientists believe that the physiological reasons for the brain's input and quantity limitations are linked to glucose consumption, synaptic adhesion, protein recycling, working memory capacity, and the hippocampus (Abel & Lattal, 2001; Bliss & Collingridge, 1993; Cambon et al., 2004; Cowan, 2001; Elgersma & Silva, 1999; Frank & Greenberg, 1994; Jensen, 2005; Jones, Sunram-Lea, & Wesnes, 2012; Kandel, 1997; Martin & Benton, 1999; Miller, 1956; Nilsson, Radeborg, & Björck, 2012; Silva, 2003; Smith & Foster, 2008; Squire, 1992; Squire & Cave, 1991). Let's look at the brain science behind input and quantity limitations and then talk about how to address these physiological challenges.

Glucose

The body does not store the brain food glucose. Given that glucose provides a significant portion of the fuel and energy to operate our cognitive architecture, when glucose is rapidly consumed and levels are low, the brain does not function at maximum capacity (Jones et al., 2012; Martin & Benton, 1999; Nilsson et al., 2012; Smith & Foster, 2008). Sustained focus on complex learning in science and mathematics depletes glucose resources, limiting the quantity of information that enters the brain. Past a certain point, the brain no longer has the fuel and energy to take in the additional information.

Synaptic Adhesion

When students learn something new, neurons get together. The dendrite of one neuron gets very close to the axon of another neuron to form a neural connection (Abel & Lattal, 2001; Cambon et al., 2004; Elgersma & Silva, 1999; Silva, 2003). This Hebbian view of neuroscience implies that knowledge and understanding are represented in the brain as a neural network of brain cells (neurons and glia cells) and brain chemicals (e.g., dopamine, serotonin, melatonin, norepinephrine; Sylwester, 2005). Thus, if a student can identify and describe the symmetries of a polynomial function as compared to a radical function, this knowledge is stored as a neural network somewhere in the student's brain. The formation of these networks takes time, in part because the neurons do not touch.

If you recall your hand model of a neuron from Chapter 2, the synapse is the gap between the dendrite of one neuron and the axon of another. Although neurons of knowledge and understanding are bundled together in a network, no two neurons touch. What holds these networks together, more specifically any two neurons, is synaptic adhesion (Cambon et al., 2004). Synaptic adhesion takes time. Too much information delivered too fast prevents the brain from pausing and processing and having time for synaptic adhesion.

Protein Recycling

Recently, protein recycling has been the focus of research on ALS or Lou Gehrig's Disease (e.g., Farr, Ying, Fenton, & Horwich, 2011). Researchers have attributed this neurodegenerative disease to misbehaving proteins that are necessary for neurons to function normally. Proteins naturally recycle through the brain and spinal cord to provide the nutrients necessary for neuronal health—more specifically, memory (Frank & Greenberg, 1994; Kandel, 1997). As with synaptic adhesion, this takes time. The "spray and pray" method starves the brain of this time, and thus, memory is impaired.

Stop-n-Think Box 6.1

Reflect on what you just read about input and quantity limitation by completing this 3-2-1 activity.

Write down three pieces of information you want to remember about glucose consumption, synaptic adhesion, and protein recycling.

1. _____
2. _____
3. _____

Write down two facts you want to share with one of your colleagues.

1. _____
2. _____

Write down one question that is lingering in your mind.

1. _____

Working Memory

In addition to glucose consumption, synaptic adhesion, and protein recycling, the brain simply does not have a lot of room in working memory. Working memory fills up! Working memory is a collection of cognitive processes, believed to be housed in the prefrontal cortex, that make it possible for the human brain to hold a limited amount of information in an active state for conscious processing (Baddeley & Hitch, 1974; Cowan et al., 2005; Cowan, Morey, Chen, Gilchrist, & Saults, 2008). This subtype of memory is what enables us to actively keep relevant information available so that we can use it to think (Conway, Cowan, & Bunting, 2001). Unfortunately, working memory is limited (Cowan, 2001; Miller, 1956).

Sticking with the food analogy, working memory is analogous to the size of the dinner plates at a buffet restaurant. The size of the plate determines how much food can be piled on a plate during a single trip to the buffet. Once the plate is full, restaurant patrons must return to their tables to "process" the food on their plates. Only then can they return to the buffet for more food. Likewise, once working memory has reached its capacity, students must stop and "process" information before taking in more information.

The Hippocampus

There is also a limit to the speed at which the brain can absorb information. The hippocampus is responsible for the slogan "too much, too fast." *Hippocampus* is Latin for "seahorse." A seahorse is exactly what the hippocampus resembles (see Figures 6.1 and 6.2).

Figure 6.1   Seahorse and Hippocampus

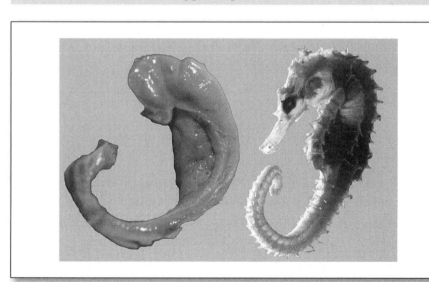

Source: Wikimedia.org.

Figure 6.2 Location of the Hippocampus

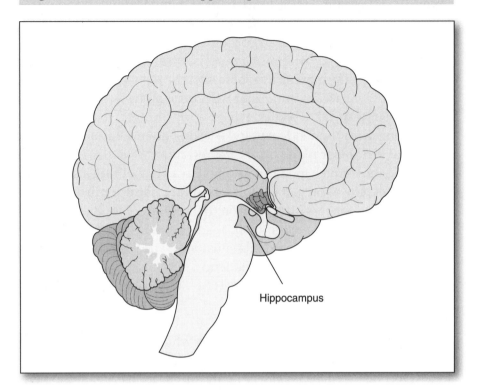

Hippocampus

The hippocampus acts as the surge protector for the brain (Jensen, 2005). Just as a surge protector prevents too much electricity from destroying your electronic devices (e.g., computer, stereo, or television), one of the many functions of the hippocampus is to prevent too much information from surging into the brain (Bliss & Collingridge, 1993; Squire, 1992; Squire & Cave, 1991). The hippocampus monitors the flow of information into the brain.

Tidbits About the Hippocampus

1. The hippocampus corresponds with the cortex to help store long-term memories.

2. The hippocampus learns quickly, but has limited capacity.

3. Too much, too fast overloads the neural circuitry of the hippocampus.

4. When overloaded, the hippocampus overwrites old information with the new information, which negatively influences learning.

5. Breaking down learning into chunks and providing students with opportunities to process the chunks at a slower rate improves retention. (Jensen, 2005)

Addressing the input and quantity limitations of the brain requires teachers to adopt a whole new perspective on how we structure our lessons. Starting class on the exact second after the tardy bell and covering content up until the dismissal bell throws too much, too fast at the student brain. In fact, when teachers use this "fire hosing" of information approach, they had better pray that when they spray the information onto the crowd of onlooking students, something sticks. Instead of "spray and pray," teachers can immediately apply the research on input and quantity limitations by breaking the class period or lesson into 10- to 12-minute segments. This approach is commonly referred to as the "press and release" method and requires teachers to chunk information together (Allen, 2001).

Press and Release

"Press and release" is an instructional approach that takes into account the input and quantity limitations of the brain. Coined by Rich Allen (2001), the concept of press and release creates the ideal ebb and flow of classroom content for the student. That is, moments of pressing or focusing on ideas, concepts, and topics should be followed by moments of release during which the student gets a chance to process and reflect. At times during the activity, lesson, or class period, students are expected to fully concentrate on taking in new information or making meaning of information. These are press situations. The length of each press phase is approximately 10 to 12 minutes or three to four chunks of information (Allen, 2001; Cowan, 2001). The release phase varies in length, depending on factors such as complexity of content, time of day, time of year, and background knowledge of the learner. Some releases are approximately a minute in length (e.g., turn to a neighbor and summarize) while others may be close to 10 minutes (e.g., develop a Venn Diagram). This cycle of press and release continues through the entire lesson or class period to ensure that the student brain conserves glucose, has time for synaptic adhesion and protein recycling, and does not overcrowd working memory or the hippocampus (see Tables 6.1 and 6.2).

In the scenarios presented in Tables 6.1 and 6.2, students in the class move through a series of presses and releases that limit the input quantity of the lesson and give students time to reflect and process learning.

An important feature of the release phase is that this pause in input is not "free time." Instead, the release phase is a pause in input

Table 6.1 Math Example of Press and Release Approach

Students work on an entrance ticket that requires them to select a problem from last night's homework and develop a written explanation of how to solve the problem. The teacher sets the timer on the SMART Board for 7 minutes.	Press
Once the timer expires, students turn to a neighbor and share the problem they selected and the written explanation. During this process, students offer feedback and make edits to their entrance ticket. The students turn in their entrance tickets by placing them in a folder at the front of the room.	Release
The teacher asks students to get out their mathematics notebooks to start the day's lesson. He or she begins by walking students through the key concepts of the day (e.g., worked examples). The students take notes.	Press
After about 10 minutes of walking students through several worked examples, the teacher asks students to develop a Venn diagram comparing and contrasting last night's homework problems with today's worked examples.	Release
The teacher presents three or four problems that students are to work on independently. The teacher moves around the room as students work independently.	Press
After 10 or 12 minutes, the teacher asks students to consult their neighbors and compare the process used and the solutions obtained from the guided practice session.	Release

Table 6.2 Science Example of Press and Release Approach

Students are asked to read silently pages 212 through 214 in their biology books.	Press
Once the teacher notices that all students have completed the brief reading task, she asks the students to make a list of the key terms presented in the reading.	Release
The teacher presents a brief lecture on cellular reproduction, meiosis. The students take notes.	Press
After approximately 10 minutes, the teacher asks the students to turn to a neighbor and alternate summarizing the last 10 minutes.	Release

The teacher asks students to develop a verbal description of the key words identified from the reading and to create a visual for each word.	Press
After 10 or 12 minutes, the teacher asks students to consult their neighbors and share their verbal descriptions and visuals for the key terms.	Release

that offers students an opportunity to reflect, review, and process the information from the press phase.

Stop-n-Think Box 6.2

Take a moment and make a list of strategies or ideas to use during the release phase of instruction. The following are a few examples.

If students' desks are arranged in groups of four, ask every student who has his or her back to the window to stand up and go sit in another student's seat and share information with the new person sitting across from him or her.
Play music and tell students to walk around the room until the music stops, give a high five to the person standing closest to them, and share their thoughts with that person.
Provide handouts to the students on different colored paper. During the release, ask students to get up and find someone else with the same color paper and share their answers or thoughts.

The content of the press phase depends on how the ideas, concepts, or topics were broken down into chunks.

Chunking

Chunking is a strategy that groups together ideas, concepts, or topics into small, meaningful units (Slavin, 2006; Visser, Plomp, Amirault, & Kuiper, 2002). The grouping of content into chunks should make sense to the teacher and to the learner. That is, chunks should be coherent bundles and not simply a collection of discrete pieces of information. These meaningful units, or chunks, should contain three to four pieces of information that can be delivered in 10- to 12-minute segments.

Have you ever completed a task analysis for a concept you were preparing to teach? A task analysis is the process of taking apart a learning task to determine the subskills or component skills needed to accomplish the task (Gagne, 1977; Gardner, 1985). Not only will this assist you in the process of "chunking" the lesson; it will also increase the probability that students will be successful during the learning process, provide an efficient way for you to monitor and adjust student learning, and will guide your ability to make valid decisions about what the next step in learning should be. This is actually the simplest way to begin to chunk the content you are teaching. As you move through the remainder of this chapter, we provide more detail.

Stop-n-Think Box 6.3

Let's start by walking through the steps of a task analysis:

1. Identify the learning objective. What do you want your students to learn? How will you know whether they have learned it?

2. Determine the subskills. Subskills are the components that are necessary for understanding the new learning.

3. Sequence the subskills in the order students need to learn them.

Now, you try!

First, select a specific topic or concept from your curriculum. Determine the subskills by brainstorming a list of essential learnings or skills needed to achieve the desired outcome (A concept map could be used to organize your list). Examine your list carefully, and sequence the items in a logical order.

Chunking information in this manner helps facilitate teaching and learning in a way that does not violate the input and quantity limitations of the brain. The chunks are delivered during the press phase of instruction.

Things to keep in mind about chunking:

1. Science and mathematics content should be delivered in small, meaningful chunks.

2. Chunks should contain three to four separate items of information.

3. Chunks are delivered during the press phase of instruction and should include a variety of strategies.

4. Chunks can include both activating background knowledge and building background knowledge.

To decide what items should be chunked together during a lesson, the teacher must start with the state or national standard associated with a specific science or mathematics unit. This process resembles the process for developing essential questions. Essential questions provide a great starting point for chunking. Let's get more specific and work through this process by revisiting the examples from Chapter 5.

Example 1: Science

Topic: The Rock Cycle

1. Earth Science Standard 6 (Virginia Standards of Learning): The student will investigate and understand the rock cycle as it relates to the origin and transformation of rock types and how to identify common rock types based on mineral composition and textures. Key concepts include

   (a)   igneous rocks;
   (b)   sedimentary rocks; and
   (c)   metamorphic rocks.

2. Important Nouns: rock cycle, origin, transformation, rock types, mineral composition, textures.

The difference between developing essential questions versus chunking information is what we do with the "important nouns." As you recall, in developing essential questions, these important nouns are translated into a summary or big idea statement and then turned into one or two essential questions (Ainsworth, 2003). When chunking information, you first arrange the important nouns into a natural learning progression. For example, the origin of rocks, rock types, mineral composition, textures, transformation, and finally the rock cycle present a learning progression. Once this progression has been established, the chunks are derived from the key understandings associated with each important noun. Table 6.3 serves as an example of chunking the rock cycle.

Table 6.3   Chunking Earth Science Standard 6

Important Nouns	Statements of Key Understandings
Origin of Rocks	Igneous rock forms from molten rock that cools and hardens either below or on Earth's surface.
	Sedimentary rocks may be formed either by rock fragments or organic matter being bound together or by chemical precipitation.
	Metamorphic rocks form when any rock is changed.
Rock Types	The processes by which rocks are formed define the three major groups of rocks.

(Continued)

Table 6.3 (Continued)

Important Nouns	Statements of Key Understandings
Mineral Composition and Texture	Rocks can be identified on the basis of mineral content and texture.
	Extrusive igneous rocks have small or no crystals, resulting in fine-grained or glassy textures.
	Intrusive igneous rocks have larger crystals and a coarser texture.
	Extrusive igneous rocks include pumice, obsidian, and basalt.
	Intrusive igneous rocks include granite.
	Sedimentary rocks are clastic or chemical.
	Clastic sedimentary rocks are made up of fragments of other rocks and include sandstone, conglomerate, and shale.
	Nonclastic sedimentary rocks include limestone and rock salt.
	Metamorphic rocks can be foliated or unfoliated (nonfoliated).
	Foliated metamorphic rocks have bands of different minerals. Slate, schist, and gneiss are foliated metamorphic rocks.
	Unfoliated metamorphic rocks have little or no banding and are relatively homogenous throughout. Marble and quartzite are unfoliated metamorphic rocks.
The Rock Cycle and Transformation of Rocks	The rock cycle is the process by which all rocks are formed and how basic Earth materials are recycled through time.

The final step is for the teacher to select the three or four specific pieces of information to present to students during the press phase of the lesson. For the preceding example, an earth science teacher may choose to further the task analysis of key understandings, depending on the learning readiness of the students. Take the key understanding associated with "The Rock Cycle and Transformation of Rocks." You may decide that the first press phase is devoted to the parts of the rock cycle while the second press phase is devoted to the characteristics of each part of the rock cycle. Finally, the teacher may devote a press phase to the transformation from one type of rock to another. The take-home message is to monitor the input and quantity limitations of the student brain. Let's revisit the mathematics example from Chapter 5.

Example 2: Geometry

Topic: Triangles

1. Geometry Standard 5 (Virginia Standards of Learning): The student, given information concerning the lengths of sides and/or measures of angles in triangles, will

    (a) order the sides by length, given the angle measures;
    (b) order the angles by degree measure, given the side lengths;
    (c) determine whether a triangle exists; and
    (d) determine the range in which the length of the third side must lie.

These concepts will be considered in the context of real-world situations.

2. Important Nouns: length, sides, measures, angles, order, degree, triangle, range.

Table 6.4   Chunking Geometry Standard 5

Important Nouns	*Statements of Key Understandings*
Lengths and Angles	Solve real-world problems given information about the lengths of sides and/or measures of angles in triangles.
	The longest side of a triangle is opposite the largest angle of the triangle and the shortest side is opposite the smallest angle.
	In a triangle, the length of two sides and the included angle determine the length of the side opposite the angle.
Order	Order the sides of a triangle by their lengths when given the measures of the angles.
	Order the angles of a triangle by their measures when given the lengths of the sides.
Lengths and Sides	Given the lengths of three segments, determine whether a triangle could be formed.
Range	Given the lengths of two sides of a triangle, determine the range in which the length of the third side must lie.
	In order for a triangle to exist, the length of each side must be within a range that is determined by the lengths of the other two sides.

Stop-n-Think Box 6.4

Now you select a specific state or national standard that you currently teach. Write that standard, including all subsections of the standard, below. As you develop this list, include the subskills needed to obtain the new learning.

_____

_____

_____

_____

Within a standard there are important nouns, like _igneous rocks_, _metamorphic rocks_, and _sedimentary rocks_, that represent the ideas, concepts, or topics students must master. Nouns are the building blocks of essential questions. Make a list of the important nouns in the standard you selected.

_____

_____

_____

_____

_____

Develop a learning progression for the important nouns.

_____

_____

_____

_____

Create a graphic organizer that maps out how you would chunk the information and key understandings associated with these nouns.

Although the chunking of material is important in monitoring input and quantity limitations, it is not unreasonable to ask, "How can we appropriately address these limitations and still get all of the material covered in our classes? How can we still cover all of the standards in this era of accountability?" There are several strategies that chunk information and monitor input and quantity limitations and still enable our students to meet and exceed the standards. Three of these strategies are discussion circles, choice boards, and the jigsaw.

Discussion Circles

A discussion circle is a cooperative learning strategy that assigns specific roles and tasks to a specific chunk of content (Daniels, 1994; Straits & Nichols, 2006; Wilfong, 2009). Although the size of each discussion circle varies and ultimately is up to the teacher, groups of three to four students are most effective (Lou, Abrami, & Spence, 2000; Lou et al., 1996; Marzano, Pickering, & Pollock, 2001). Table 6.5 provides examples of discussion circle roles and tasks and includes discussion directors, summarizers, word wizard, mapmaker, and highlighter (Howard, 2010a, 2010b; Johnson & Johnson, 1999; Wilfong, 2012). The roles used in a specific discussion circle depend on the nature of the content and the objectives for that particular lesson.

Table 6.5 Discussion Circle Roles and Tasks

Discussion Circle Role	Task
Discussion Director or Leader	Direct, lead, or guide the activities in the discussion circle. Decide the presentation order for each group member and his or her task. Develop a set of critical thinking questions (not yes, no, or one-word response questions) that encourage group members to make connections between the content, current events, other class topics, and/or group members' lives.
Big Idea Builder or Summarizer	Develops a list of the big ideas or the "must knows" for the content. Creates a visual or written summary of the content. Prepares a response to the question, "Why is this material important?"

(Continued)

Table 6.5 (Continued)

Discussion Circle Role	Task
Word Wizard	Identifies key vocabulary, terms, or concepts.
	Prepares a description of each vocabulary, term, or concept.
	Creates a visual for each item.
	Identifies a specific example of each item.
	The word wizard provides locations or further information about each vocabulary, term, or concept.
Map Maker	Creates a concept map of the material.
	Explains why certain concepts are connected together on the concept map.
Highlighter	Identifies important readings, sections, or passages.
	Marks these passages with a sticky note or tab.
	Justifies why particular readings, sections, or passages were selected.

Once students are assigned to groups and their individual roles are determined, the teacher should provide ample time for the completion of individual tasks. How students are grouped is ultimately up to the teacher. However, research suggests that students should be grouped using a variety of criteria (e.g., random selection, interest, birthday month, alphabetically, colors in their clothing, and ability) and have the opportunity to work in different groups throughout the school year (Lou et al., 1996, 2000; Slavin, 1987a, 1987b). As a word of caution, grouping based on ability level should be used sparingly because it produces mixed results. Put differently, low-ability students often experience a negative outcome from homogenous grouping (Lou et al., 1996, 2000).

Take a reading assignment in any science or mathematics class (e.g., a chapter on classification in biology, a section on periodic trends in chemistry, a section on matrix operations in algebra, or the section on the geometric representation of polar coordinates). Once students have an explicit purpose for reading, they are more likely to engage in the reading task (Howard, 2010a, 2010b). Assigning students to a discussion circle and having them select a role provides a behaviorally relevant reason for actively reading the science or mathematics material.

How to Conduct a Discussion Circle

1. Pre-assign groups of three or four students. These groups can be random, homogeneous, or heterogeneous (e.g., based on ability, interest).

2. Within each group, assign students their individual roles or empower students to select a role.

3. Identify the content that is the focus of the discussion circle (e.g., reading selection, concept, topic, idea, or problem set).

4. Provide time for students to individually complete the task associated with their role.

5. After a time, instruct students to take turns presenting their tasks to the other members of their group.

Discussion circles provide an opportunity for students to engage with a larger quantity of content without overloading the input and quantity components of the brain. What alleviates the pressure on glucose consumption, synaptic adhesion, protein recycling, working memory, and the hippocampus is that students are individually responsible for a specific role and task. The role and task require each group member to consolidate information or content in a different way. This, in turn, helps the students consolidate large quantities of information into smaller, more digestible chunks. The sharing component of discussion circles provides an additional opportunity for students to hear about the roles and tasks of fellow group members. One of the powerful ways to increase learning and retention is to teach someone else (Medina, 2008). This should not be overlooked as teachers engage their students in this cooperative learning activity.

Stop-n-Think Box 6.5

Take a minute to think about the use of discussion circles in your classroom. Elaborate on the following questions.

1. What specific content do you teach that would align with the use of discussion circles?

2. What would be the most effective way to group your students for discussion circles on that topic?

3. What individual roles would you utilize during this activity? How would those roles be assigned?

4. How much time would you allow for each individual to complete his or her work?

5. How do you see this instructional strategy benefiting the learning in your classroom?

Choice Boards

Just as the name suggests, choice boards are a menu of options from which students select a topic or task for processing science or mathematics content (Gregory & Chapman, 2008; Gregory & Hammerman, 2008). This is a variation of the choice board you read about in Chapter 5. As students enter the room, they sign up under the topic or task that they are interested in engaging in for the lesson or class period. Let's look at two examples. Table 6.6 is a choice board in which the choices are physics topics.

Table 6.6   Physics Choice Board

Topic	Sign Up
First Law of Thermodynamics	1. 2. 3. 4.
Thermodynamic Processes	1. 2. 3. 4.
Reversible and Irreversible Processes	1. 2. 3. 4.
Efficiency	1. 2. 3. 4.
The Carnot Cycle	1. 2. 3. 4.
Entropy	1. 2. 3. 4.

This particular choice board is for a class of 24 students. Once students have signed up, as a group of four they are responsible for developing an understanding of the material and completing the tasks given. The group is also informed that they will be responsible to teach the concept to the whole class. The teacher has lots of flexibility when designing each task. The assignments could contain a wide range of tasks, from concrete to abstract, low to high levels of thinking skills, or even ranges in the levels of creativity involved in completing the task. As mentioned in Chapter 5, choice boards really open the door to differentiation.

Table 6.7 is a mathematics example in which the choices are tasks and the topic is matrix addition and scalar multiplication. Students sign up for the task of their choice and work cooperatively to complete the task. After completing the task, students share their work with the whole class.

Table 6.7   Math Choice Board

Topic: Matrix Addition and Scalar Multiplication	Sign Up
Develop a set of worked examples with written narratives explaining how to work each example.	1. 2. 3. 4.
Develop a brochure that provides an overview of the topic.	1. 2. 3. 4.
Prepare a presentation on the application of matrix addition and scalar multiplication.	1. 2. 3. 4.
Create an assessment.	1. 2. 3. 4.

(Continued)

Table 6.7 (Continued)

Topic: Matrix Addition and Scalar Multiplication	Sign Up
Create an instruction video clip explaining matrix addition and scalar multiplication.	1. 2. 3. 4.
Develop a set of fill-in notes for this topic.	1. 2. 3. 4.

Stop-n-Think Box 6.6

Now you try it. Develop a topic and a task choice board for an upcoming class. Once you have completed the choice board, reflect on the following questions:

1. What was your rationale for the topic you selected?

2. Is the choice board you designed teacher directed or student centered?

3. How did you embed individual accountability to ensure high levels of active participation?

Jigsaw

The jigsaw strategy is a cooperative learning strategy that relies on an expert group and a base group. The jigsaw is particularly effective for covering more material in less time while still respecting the input and quantity limitations of the brain (Aronson, Blaney, Stephan, Sikes, & Snapp, 1978; Gregory & Chapman, 2008; Gregory & Hammerman, 2008; Slavin, 1994). Students are assigned to an expert group, similar to the discussion groups, in which they develop expertise in a particular idea, concept, or topic. Each member understands that he or she will be responsible to share the knowledge he or she has gained with the larger group. For example, the teacher might develop expert groups on each application of the derivative (i.e., related rates, mean value, critical points, graphing, maximization and minimization problems, and differential equations). In science, an expert group could be developed for each type of map (i.e., bathymetric, geologic, topographic, weather, and star chart). After an allotted amount of time, students return to their base groups and teach the material to the other members of the base group.

Let's take a closer look at how to implement a jigsaw in your classroom.

1. Select the topic of learning. Divide the topic into learnable chunks. The number of chunks will depend on the specific content and the number of expert groups needed.

2. If necessary, refer to and use the process of task analysis described earlier in this chapter.

3. Divide the students into expert groups. Inform each group of the chunk they are to become experts in. Embed measures of accountability to ensure that hesitant learners will become actively engaged in complex material.

4. Assign students to base groups. The number of students in each base group is equal to the number of expert groups, and each base group member is also a member of a different expert group.

5. Have students review the expert material individually.

6. Have students meet and collaborate in their expert group.

7. Provide group support for material that may be difficult to master alone, and help students master content in greater depth without violating input and quantity limitations.

8. Provide time for expert groups to complete the activity and prepare their teaching strategy.

9. Have experts return to their base group and teach.

Discussion circles, choice boards, and jigsaws are only three examples of chunking content in a way that respects the input and quantity limitations of the human brain. There are many others. One common characteristic of these three strategies is that each one provides a meaningful way for students to actively engage in content above and beyond the traditional lecture format. This is not to say that lecture is off limits. There are times when teachers have to clarify and share insights with students. The important thing to remember is that students must have time to release from high focus and concentration. Whether it is a jigsaw, lecture, or sustained reading task, the quantity of input should be limited. Breaking down the activity, lesson, or class period into 10- to 12-minute segments helps prevent reaching the limit and causing the students to disengage simply because they are on overload. However, the time between segments is just as important in terms of processing, reviewing, and reflecting on the previous learning segment. This time between chunks is not free time!

What to Do Between Chunks?

Think-Pair-Share

After a press situation that involves the presentation of a short body of content, pause and let students release from this segment of concentration. Have each student review the content from the previous segment. This might include reading over their notes, thumbing through a reading passage associated with the content, reviewing a worked example, or looking over a visual or diagram. After a minute or two, have students turn to a neighbor and summarize the information contained in the notes, reading passage, worked example, or visual. Ask students to identify and highlight critical points. This think-pair-share moment of release should take about three to four minutes. Once students appear to be wrapping up their conversations or moving on to extraneous topics, stop them and provide an opportunity for them to ask questions.

Although the think-pair-share strategy works in many situations, like video clips, demonstrations, or homework, it is particularly effective in segmenting or chunking a lecture. If a direct-instruction-style lecture is the method of delivery for a particular topic, stop and release about every 10 to 12 minutes. As students become more familiar with this approach, you will see an increase in the quality of questions and note taking by the students.

Personal Response Systems

A second idea for the release phase is the use of instructional technology. No doubt about it, end-of-course tests that are populated with multiple-choice items are inevitable. Personal response systems or clickers provide an opportunity for students to get a release and engage in test-taking practice. After the presentation of a chunk or segment of material, provide students with a multiple-choice question. Ideally, this question would be a released item from a previous end-of-course test. Before students are allowed to respond, they must talk with their neighbors to both share their answers and justify their selection. As an example, an algebra teacher might present a multiple-choice problem after working through several examples of solving and graphing inequalities.

In the event that a classroom does not have access to a personal response system, students could write their answers on small dry erase boards or use hand responses: Instead of writing A, B, C, or D, have students hold up 1, 2, 3, or 4 fingers to indicate their response.

Cubing

Cubing is a release strategy for processing, reviewing, and reflecting on previous chunks of information. Cubing can be done as a whole-group task or as a small-group and partnering task. To get started, the teacher identifies an idea, concept, or topic from the previous learning segment. Students engage in the cubing strategy by rolling the cube and answering the question written on the cube, either verbally or by keeping a written record of their responses in a notebook (see Figure 6.3).

Figure 6.3   An Astronomy Cube

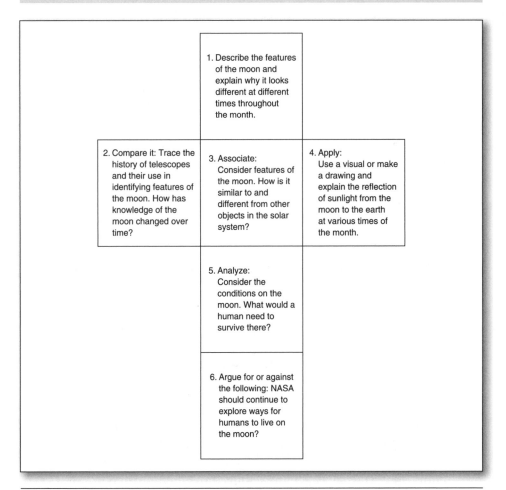

Source: Gregory and Hammerman (2008, Figure 51, p. 136). Used with permission.

As an example, students in a 10th-grade biology class just finished a 12-minute lecture on the nutrient cycling and energy flow in ecosystems. The teacher pauses and asks students to make a list of the key terms presented in the last learning segment. A minute or two later, the teacher asks the students to select one term from their list and put an asterisk or star beside the term. After students have arranged their chairs into small groups of two or three according to the term they put an asterisk next to, the teacher distributes cubes to each group.

How to Use the Cubing Strategy

1. Cubes can be made using a square box or students can make them from card stock or cardboard. Templates for cubes can be found online.

2. Students design or select six questions about the topic they are given. There are examples in the next list.

3. Write one question or task on each side of the cube. (Hint: If you are using the templates found online, it is easier to write the questions on the cube before cutting out and folding it.)

4. Tape or glue the template together, or if you are using a premade box, tape or glue squares of paper to each side of the box.

5. Have students roll the cube and complete the "rolled" task in their science notebooks.

6. Continue this activity for approximately five minutes and then move on to the next 12-minute segment.

The following are examples of cubing questions. "It" refers to the previous chunk or one idea, concept, or topic within the previous chunk.

Describe it (What are the major characteristic or points?)

Compare it (This is like . . .)

Analyze it (What can you do with it?)

Apply it (How does it relate to the "real world"?)

Connect it (What is it similar to? What is it different from?)

Illustrate it (Create a visual of it.)

Write it (Develop a definition of it using your own words.)

Rearrange it (e.g., In math, rearrange the formula for a specific variable.)

Question it (Write a question about it.)

Cubing allows students to examine an issue or topic from a variety of different angles while hearing the different perspectives of their classmates. There are many ways to design the cubing strategy that will result in differentiated learning for your students. The tasks or questions can be designed using different levels of thinking, multiple intelligences, or according to the students' readiness levels. Asking students to design cubes for classroom activities often results in an improvement in their ability to create thought-provoking questions.

Too Much, Too Fast

This part of the recipe is all about the presentation of material. A marinade covers the piece of red meat, chicken, or pork in a flavorful liquid that adds flavor and makes the food more digestible. It is analagous to the way content should be covered during the learning process. Science and mathematics content should be covered in a cognitively delectable experience that makes the information appealing and mentally consumable and digestible. However, the brain cannot withstand a long marinating process. Although red meat, chicken, or pork often improves the longer it soaks in the marinade, the human brain likes 10- to 12-minute segments of marinating. Too much, too fast overloads the brain and exceeds the input and quantity limitations. Therefore, to keep students engaged, input should be broken down into 10- to 12-minute segments that alternate between moments of pressing and moments of releasing.

CHAPTER 6: EXIT TICKET

Chunk the information form this chapter using a Donut Organizer (see Figure 6.4). Select one of the key ideas or strategies from this chapter and write it in the center of the donut. Fill in the outer ring with details from the chapter or your personal experiences.

Photo from Thinkstock.com.

Figure 6.4   Donut Organizer

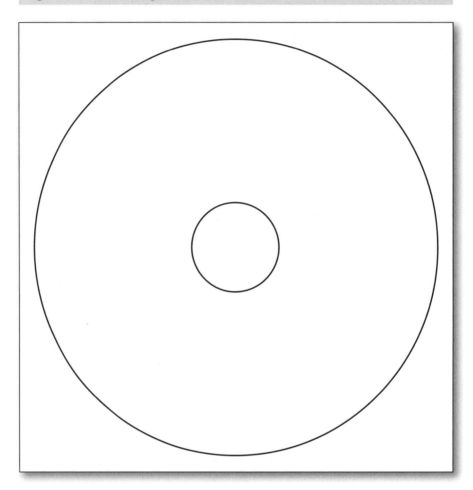

Engaging Professional Development Tasks

1. This professional development task involves chunking content in your classroom. Select a unit or topic that is traditionally the most cognitively complex area in your class. Using any and all available resources (e.g., curriculum documents, textbook, feedback from previous years, or colleagues who teach the same course) and break the topic down into what you think is a logical progression of smaller chunks. Create a concept map that shows the progression of student learning through the unit or topic. Use the following

questions to guide the development of your learning chunks and concept map:

- What concepts or skills in the unit or topic were most challenging to the previous students?
- Can the chunks be delivered in 10- to 12-minute learning segments?
- Do the chunks follow a natural progression through the unit or topic?
- How did you decide what the chunks were and how different topics were grouped together?

2. This professional development task involves a second video critique of your teaching. Video record yourself teaching a lesson or activity or use the same video from the professional development task in Chapter 1. If you are video recording a second lesson, set up the flip camera or digital video recorder. Watch your teaching video by yourself to ensure an honest evaluation and critique. Make notes of what you observe during this teaching episode. Use the following questions to guide your reflection about your teaching video:

- What general observations did you make about the amount of content covered in the lesson?
- How many ideas, concepts, or topics did you cover in the lesson?
- Did you segment learning in the lesson? If so, how long were your segments?
- How did you use the technique of "press and release"?
- What strategies did you use to encourage students to process and reflect on chunks of learning?
- How has this video review and reflection changed your perspective on input limitations of the student brain?

References

Abel, T., & Lattal, K. M. (2001). Molecular mechanisms of memory acquisition, consolidation and retrieval. *Current Opinion in Neurobiology, 11,* 180–187.

Ainsworth, L. (2003). *Unwrapping the standards: A simple process to make standards manageable.* Englewood, CO: Lead + Learn Press.

Allen, R. H. (2001). *Impact teaching: Ideas and strategies for teachers to maximize student learning.* Boston: Allyn & Bacon.

Aronson, E., Blaney, N., Stephan, C., Sikes, J., & Snapp, M. (1978). *The jigsaw classroom*. Beverly Hills, CA: Sage.

Baddeley, A. (1999). *Essentials of human memory*. Philadelphia: Psychology Press.

Baddeley, A., & Hitch, G. (1974). Working memory. In G. H. Bower (Ed.), *The psychology of learning and motivation: Advances in research and theory* (Vol. 8, pp. 47—90). New York: Academic Press.

Bliss, T. V. P., & Collingridge, G. L. (1993). A synaptic model of memory: Long-term potentiation in the hippocampus. *Nature, 361,* 31–39.

Cambon, K., Hansen, S. M., Venero, C., Herrero, A. I., Skibo, G., Berezin, V., . . . Sandi, C. (2004). A synthetic neural cell adhesion molecule mimetic peptide promotes synaptogenesis, enhances presynaptic function, and facilitates memory consolidation. *The Journal of Neuroscience, 24*(17), 4197–4204.

Conway, A. R. A., Cowan, N., & Bunting, M. F. (2001). The cocktail party phenomenon revisited: The importance of working memory capacity. *Psychonomic Bulletin & Review, 8*(2), 331–335.

Cowan, N. (2001). The magical number 4 in short-term memory: A reconsideration of mental storage capacity. *Behavioral and Brain Sciences, 24,* 87–185.

Cowan, N., Elliott, E. M., Saults, J. S., Morey, C. C., Mattox, S., Hismjatullina, A., & Conway, A. R. A. (2005). On the capacity of attention: Its estimation and its role in working memory and cognitive aptitudes. *Cognitive Psychology, 51,* 42–100.

Cowan, N., Morey, C. C., Chen, Z., Gilchrist, A. L., & Saults, J. S. (2008). Theory and measurement of working memory capacity limits. *The Psychology of Learning and Motivation, 49,* 49–104.

Daniels, H. (1994). *Literature circles: Voice and choice in the student-centered classroom*. Portland, ME: Stenhouse.

Elgersma, Y., & Silva, A. J. (1999). Molecular mechanisms of synaptic plasticity and memory. *Current Opinion in Neurobiology, 9,* 209–213.

Ericcson, K. A., & Kintsch, W. (1995). Long-term working memory. *Psychological Review, 102,* 211–245.

Farr, G. W., Ying, Z., Fenton, W. A., & Horwich, A. L. (2011). Hydrogen-deuterium exchange in vivo to measure turnover of an ALS-associated mutant SOD1 protein in spinal cord of mice. *Protein Science, 20*(10), 1692–1696.

Frank, D. A., & Greenberg, M. E. (1994). CREB: A mediator of long-term memory from mollusks to mammals. *Cell, 79,* 5–8.

Gagne, R. (1977). *The conditions of learning* (3rd ed.). New York: Holt, Rinehart and Winston.

Gardner, M. K. (1985). Cognitive psychological approaches to instructional task analysis. In E. W. Gordon (Ed.), *Review of research in education* (Vol. 12, pp. 157–195). Washington, DC: American Educational Research Association.

Gregory, G., & Chapman, C. (2008). *Differentiated instructional strategies. One size doesn't fit all* (2nd ed.). Thousand Oaks, CA: Corwin.

Gregory, G., & Hammerman, E. (2008). *Differentiated instructional strategies for science grades K-8*. Thousand Oaks, CA: Corwin.

Howard, L. (2010a). *Five easy steps to a balanced science program for secondary grades.* Englewood, CO: Lead + Learn Press.

Howard, L. (2010b). *Five easy steps to a balanced science program for upper elementary and middle school grades.* Englewood, CO: Lead + Learn Press.

Jensen, E. (2005). *Teaching with the brain in mind* (2nd ed.). Alexandria, VA: Association for Supervision and Curriculum Development.

Johnson, D. W., & Johnson, R. T. (1999). *Learning together and alone: Cooperative, competitive, and individualistic learning.* Boston: Allyn & Bacon.

Jones, E. K., Sunram-Lea, S. I., & Wesnes, K. A. (2012). Acute ingestion of different macronutrients differentially enhances aspects of memory and attention in healthy young adults. *Biological Psychology, 89,* 477–486.

Kandel, E. R. (1997). Genes, synapses, and long-term memory. *Journal of Cell Physiology, 173,* 124–125.

Lou, Y., Abrami, P. C., & Spence, J. C. (2000). Effects of within-class grouping on student achievement: An exploratory model. *The Journal of Educational Research, 94*(2), 101–112.

Lou, Y., Abrami, P. C., Spence, J. C., Poulsen, C., Chambers, B., & d'Apollonia, S. (1996). Within-class grouping: A meta-analysis. *Review of Educational Research, 66*(4), 423–458.

Martin, P. Y., & Benton, D. (1999). The influence of a glucose drink on a demanding working memory task. *Physiology & Behavior, 67*(1), 69–74.

Marzano, R. J., Pickering, D. J., & Pollock, J. E. (2001). *Classroom instruction that works. Research-based strategies for increasing student achievement.* Alexandria, VA: Association for Supervision and Curriculum Development.

Medina, J. (2008). *Brain rules. 12 principles for surviving and thriving at work, home, and school.* Seattle, WA: Pear Press.

Miller, G. A. (1956). The magical number seven, plus or minus two: Some limits on our capacity for processing information. *Psychological Review, 63,* 81–97.

Nilsson, A., Radeborg, K., & Björck, I. (2012). Effects on cognitive performance of modulating the postprandial blood glucose profile at breakfast. *European Journal of Clinical Nutrition, 66,* 1039–1043.

Silva, A. J. (2003). Molecular and cellular cognitive studies of the role of synaptic plasticity in memory. *Journal of Neurobiology, 54,* 224–237.

Slavin, R. E. (1987a). Ability grouping and student achievement in the elementary school: A best-evidence synthesis. *Review of Educational Research, 57,* 293–336.

Slavin, R. E. (1987b). Grouping for instruction in the elementary school. *Educational Psychologist, 22,* 89–109.

Slavin, R. E. (1994). *Using student team learning* (4th ed.). Baltimore, MD: Johns Hopkins University, Center for Research on Elementary and Middle Schools.

Slavin, R. E. (2006). *Educational psychology. Theory and practice* (8th ed.). Boston: Pearson Education.

Smith, M. A., & Foster, J. K. (2008). Glucoregulatory and order effects on verbal episodic memory in healthy adolescents after oral glucose administration. *Biological Psychology, 79,* 209–215.

Squire, L. R. (1992). Memory and the hippocampus: A synthesis from findings with rats, monkeys, and humans. *Psychological Review, 99*(2), 195–231.

Squire, L. R., & Cave, C. B. (1991). The hippocampus, memory, and space. *Hippocampus, 1*(3), 269–271.

Straits, W., & Nichols, S. (2006). Literature circles for science. *Science and Children, 44*(3), 52–55.

Sylwester, R. (2005). *How to explain a brain. An educator's handbook of brain terms and cognitive processes.* Thousand Oaks, CA: Corwin.

Visser, L., Plomp, T., Amirault, R., & Kuiper, W. (2002). Motivating students at a distance: The case of an international audience. *Educational Technology Research & Development, 50*(2), 94–110.

Wilfong, L. G. (2009). Textmasters: Bringing literature circles to textbook reading across the curriculum. *Journal of Adolescent & Adult Literacy, 53*(2): 164–171.

Wilfong, L. G. (2012). The science text for all. Using textmasters to help all students access written science content. *Science Scope, 35*(5), 56–63.

7

Make Learning a Long-Lasting, Invigorating Experience

Stop-n-Think Box 7.1

What specific strategies do you use to help students learn the material in your class? How do you help students make learning stick?

Our understanding of home-cooked meals is populated by instant dinners in the freezer section of our local supermarket. In some cases, these instant dinners are from our favorite restaurants (e.g., T.G.I. Friday's or P.F. Chang's). Americans have grown accustomed to coming home, throwing a packaged meal into the microwave or convection oven, leaving it unattended, and in less than an hour the meal is ready to eat. Our busy schedules make this variation of home cooking both convenient and necessary. We sit around these packaged meals and reminisce about the days our grandparents, parents, or acquaintances spent hours, or even the entire day, preparing a meal. In fact, someone always had to stay close by the oven or stovetop to monitor the progress of each component of the meal. This likely involved sticking a fork into the poultry or red meat dish, sticking a knife or toothpick into a side dish, or quickly stirring and tasting the stovetop dish. After all, undercooked chicken; dried-up macaroni and cheese; and unseasoned, overcooked green beans make for a less than delectable dinner.

Learning works the same way! Making learning a long-lasting and invigorating experience takes a significant amount of monitoring. As teachers, we cannot walk into a classroom, get out a package of content for the lesson or activity, throw it out to students, leave it unmonitored or unchecked for the class period, and count on it being ready when the dismissal bell rings. When it comes to learning in the classroom, the adolescent brain—any brain, for that matter—needs monitoring. The most challenging part of this characteristic of the adolescent brain is that students do not know that they need monitoring.

It's as if They Were Never Even in Class

How often have you stood in front of a classroom full of students, observed the looks on their faces, and just known they had questions? Did you find yourself asking, "Are there any questions?" and as you glanced around the room, several students whispered, "No," while others had no response at all? Did you accept their lack of response as confirmation that they understood the content of the lesson? On the flip side, have you ever experienced a sense of relief when students did not ask any questions? If the students don't have questions, your amazing planning and teaching must have worked like a charm. Without a moment of hesitation you moved on with instruction. After all, we have to get through the standards before the end-of-course assessment, and if there are no questions, then content must be sticking. Unfortunately, several days later you administered an assessment and found yourself thinking, "It's as if they were never in the class or never heard this stuff before."

Stop-n-Think Box 7.2

What factors influence student retention in your classroom? What classroom strategies are you currently using that contribute to student retention?

Believe it or not, in the scenarios above, the brain is doing exactly what was designed to do. The very frustrating experience described above is only one example of the behavioral evidence supporting what brain researchers (i.e., Glickman, 1961; Loftus, 1979; McGaugh, 1966, 2000; Polster, Nadel, & Schacter, 1991; Squire, 1992; Squire, Cohen, & Nadel, 1984; Wiltgen, Brown, Talton, & Silva, 2004) conceptualize as three behaviors of the brain related to learning and the consolidation of memories:

- Initial learning, or memory, is very fragile and vulnerable to forgetting or distortion.
- The brain rarely gets learning right the first time.
- What the brain thinks about, it remembers.

Science and mathematics teachers are not able to change the physiological functions of the brain that have long been a part of our evolutionary trajectory. However, we can beat the adolescent brain at its own game, as long as we know the rules by which that three-pound teenage enigma is playing.

Forgetting

On any given day, the brain produces approximately 70,000 thoughts. In addition to generating these thoughts, the sensory neurons of the brain take in approximately 60,000 stimuli per second (Jensen, 2005). Therefore, our brain cannot process or remember everything that it encounters. If the human brain did take on this challenge, our heads would explode. To prevent being flooded by stimuli, which would lead to a complete brain shut down, a physiological system of checks and balances has developed that either blocks out the stimuli completely, not allowing them to register in the brain, or takes the information in as a rough draft and waits for environmental cues over time to signal that the information is worth remembering (McGaugh, 2000; Medina, Bekinschtein, Cammarota, & Izquierdo, 2008; Wolfe, 2010). This time-dependent process of memory consolidation is highly relevant to teachers and the focus of this chapter.

Is This Worth Remembering?

In the classroom, the student brain makes a decision, based on feedback and environmental cues, whether to hold onto information and move the mathematics or science concepts into long-term memory or simply forget these ideas. Feedback and various environmental cues come in the form of many of the ideas presented in previous chapters (i.e., links to prior knowledge, novelty, relevancy, pace, and quantity of input; Morris, 2006; Tse et al., 2011; van Kesteren, Fernandez, Norris, & Hermans, 2010; van Kesteren, Rijpkema, Ruiter, & Fernandez, 2010; van Kesteren, Ruiter, Fernandez, & Henson, 2012; Wang & Morris, 2010). Specific to this chapter is the idea that the brain takes in a highly malleable rough draft of the learning, and it is our responsibility to implement strategies (more environmental cues) and provide feedback that signals to the brain that the information needs to be consolidated and moved to long-term storage.

Stop-n-Think Box 7.3

Make a list of the ideas, concepts, or topics in a particular unit or class that have required a significant amount of reteaching. Reflect on the reasons you believe your students often forget the items on this list.

As students take in information about the Laws of Thermodynamics, monomials, binomials, or polynomials, the brain develops neuronal representations of the input in the hippocampus (Figure 7.1; Frankland & Bontempi, 2005; McClelland, McNaughton, & O'Reilly, 1995; Squire & Alvarez, 1995).

The hippocampus temporarily holds on to these neuronal representations for at least two reasons: (1) to decide whether or not the

Figure 7.1   Location of the Hippocampus

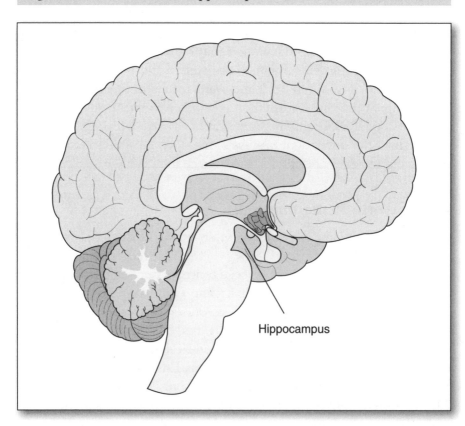

information is worth storing in long-term memory and (2) to check whether the cortical regions recognize any of the representations as familiar, thus reemphasizing the importance of background and prior knowledge (Lewis & Durrant, 2011; Medina et al., 2008; Morris, 2006; Tse et al., 2011). With regard to reason (2), if the hippocampus gets a thumbs-up from other cortical regions, indicating that the information is familiar, the hippocampus passes the recognized content along and takes on the next set of neuronal representations. This process takes time! It is reason (1) that needs a closer look and relates to the idea that the brain is not designed to get learning right the first time.

Rough Drafts

The first time a student experiences content in the science or mathematics classroom, the brain takes in a cognitive rough draft of the information (Glickman, 1961; Loftus, 1979; McGaugh, 1966, 2000; Polster et al., 1991; Squire, 1992; Takashima et al., 2006; Wiltgen et al., 2004). A cognitive rough draft is analogous to the rough draft of a paper in a high school English or Social Studies classroom. The cognitive rough draft is unedited, often laced with mistakes or inaccuracies, and is peppered with holes or gaps in the content. The concept of a cognitive rough draft pertains to the neuronal representations that are in a temporary holding pattern in the hippocampus (Frankland & Bontempi, 2005). The initial development of these neuronal representations provides the gist of the new learning, but the brain has yet to fill in the details or secure a spot for the learning in long-term memory. Again, this takes time.

The elimination of rough drafts and the fragile initial learning and memories is quite manageable if we remember that what the brain thinks about, it remembers.

Thinking Leads to Remembering

This brain idea is simple. When students have to think about an idea, concept, or topic, the brain is alerted that the information may be worth remembering (Willingham, 2009). Dan Willingham refers to memory as "the residue of thought." That is, thinking about something activates the neural circuitry, giving it a higher priority for transition into long-term memory. In addition, the specific thoughts help revise the rough draft of the idea, concept, or topic that has just been flagged as worth remembering. Consider the following scenarios.

1. A chemistry teacher has decided to help her students avoid forgetting and fill in their rough drafts. She believes that repetition is a good approach. She assigns 25 reduction-oxidation problems for homework.

2. An earth science teacher has decided to have his students copy the definitions of the vocabulary words for the oceans unit. He then asks the students to make flash cards and review them every night.

3. An algebra teacher works 10 examples of single-variable equations on the board and has his students copy them into their notebooks.

4. In a trigonometry class, a teacher assigns 10 problems focusing on trigonometric identities every night, in addition to homework.

Each of the four preceding scenarios is an example of how a science or mathematics teacher might encourage his or her students to think. Although the specifics of each scenario vary, the underlying idea is that repetition encourages students to think about the content, and thus, they are more likely to remember and revise their mental rough drafts. This assumption makes sense, and the tasks above are reasonable next steps to addressing forgetting, rough drafts, and thinking to remember. However, consider the next scenario, involving our smallest denomination of currency, the penny. Of the 15 pennies in the following picture, only one is the correct image of a penny. Can you find it?

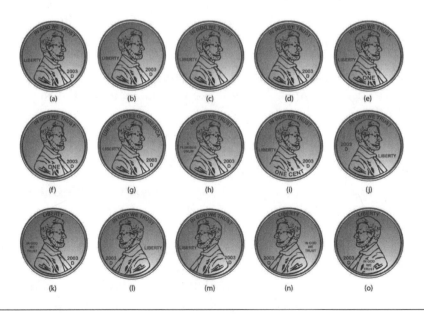

Source: © Exploratorium, www.exploratorium.edu.

Suffice it to say, this was no easy task. In fact, you more than likely had to locate a real penny to verify your answer (which is *a*). However, we have all seen hundreds, if not thousands, of pennies in our lifetime. So clearly, repetition alone is not the answer to helping students; otherwise, you would be able to draw a perfect penny from memory. Similarly, completing an assignment of a "gazillion" physics or mathematics problems or reviewing a mile-high stack of bones in the skeletal system is not going to make learning a long-lasting experience.

Stop-n-Think Box 7.4

Reflect on the assignments you have given your students. Do your assignments, in class and for homework, require your students to think? Are there adjustments you could make to produce tasks that are more thought provoking?

The activities and assignments in science and mathematics classrooms must require a level of thinking beyond simply "going through the motions" (Wolfe, 2010). You have frequently looked at a penny, but you were thinking about something else besides characteristics that would have led you to correctly select choice *a* in the preceding example. So how do we get students to think about the right stuff? This task begins with checking for understanding.

Checking for Understanding

Checking for understanding is a systematic approach used to monitor and adjust daily instruction based on student responses. An essential component of academic success involves both the teacher and the student actively and continuously monitoring student learning using specific strategies designed to gather information. In the end, checks for understanding are designed and implemented to decrease forgetting, fill in rough drafts, and encourage students to think about ideas, concepts, or topics in a way that makes learning a long-lasting experience.

These strategies can range in complexity as well as intensity. You must keep the end in mind. Can you articulate the desired outcome? Do you know specifically what you want your students to learn? You will find that the smaller the chunk of time between your checks, the more specific the learning outcomes. Consequently, the more directly and quickly you can obtain the necessary information, the better. Three examples of checks for understanding are (1) active student responding, (2) active reading, and (3) closure.

Active Student Responding

Active student responding is a group of strategies that encourage—and even require—students to respond to questions during an activity or lesson (Gettinger & Walter, 2012). Active student responses must be observable, measurable, and easily detected by teacher or student. Some common strategies for active student responding are choral responses, response cards, value line-ups, and fill-in notes.

Choral Responses

Choral responses are moments during instruction when the teacher either asks a question or prompts the students to all respond at once (Becker & Carnine, 1980; Hunter, 1982; Rosenshine & Stevens, 1986). Choral responses are like verbal fill-in-the-blank questions. For each of the following examples, the teacher would verbally provide the root statement and pause for students to verbally fill in the blank as a whole class. This strategy is most effective when it is paired with a cue from the teacher (e.g., the teacher cups his or her ear and points toward the students or provides a hint like "It starts with an *a*; it's . . .").

Choral Response Examples

1. The sine is equal to the (teacher pauses and points to students, encouraging them to say "opposite") over the (teacher pauses again and points to students, encouraging them to say "hypotenuse").

2. Newton's Second Law of Motion is written mathematically as F equals m (teacher pauses and points to students, encouraging them to say "times a").

The missing word or phrase that you want students to chorally respond with should be the big idea or concept associated with the activity or lesson. When students realize that they will be asked to chorally respond throughout a lesson, they often will be more attentive and engaged, in anticipation of such moments (McKenzie, 1979; McKenzie & Henry, 1979).

Response Cards

Response cards are either prewritten or blank cards that students use to respond to questions by the teacher. Prewritten cards are designed for specific units or have a specific purpose. For example, each of the students in a high school biology class has four laminated cards at his or her lab table. The cards are labeled A, B, C, and D. Throughout the class period, the teacher puts up one or two multiple-choice questions about the chunk of content that was just presented. The teacher informs the students that they have 90 seconds to hold up a response. The teacher checks to see whether students are arriving at the correct answer. This provides the teacher with immediate feedback about student learning.

An alternative to this approach would be to have students discuss the possible answers with their neighbors and then make a decision.

A Mathematics Example of Prewritten Response Cards

Mrs. Smith finds it very beneficial to obtain choral responses from her math students. She truly tries to achieve 100% active participation as often as possible. When you walk into her room, you will often find colored strips of paper with various concepts printed on them (e.g., vertical angles, complimentary angles, supplementary angles, adjacent angles) in the middle of students' tables. As Mrs. Smith presents a series of concepts or statements, she asks the students to respond by holding up the appropriate strip of colored paper. For example, a student would hold up the red strip if the answer is "vertical angles," the blue strip if the answer is "complimentary angles," green if the answer is "supplementary angles," and yellow if the answer is "adjacent angles." Mrs. Smith lets the students know that her statement may correspond to more than one type of angle.

Sample statements:

- Angles that are formed by two intersecting lines.
- Angles that are congruent and share a common vertex.
- Any two angles such that the sum of their measures is 90°.
- Any two angles such that the sum of their measures is 180°.
- Any two non-overlapping angles that share a common side and a common vertex.

As Mrs. Smith observes the student responses, she can see which students have a solid understanding of these types of angles.

Blank response cards are common practice in mathematics classes. Laminated sheets of white paper make reusable response cards. On this paper, or on an 8" × 8" whiteboard square, students use a dry erase marker to write their answers to a teacher-initiated question; then answers can be quickly shared with the teacher. Response cards work just as effectively in science classrooms.

Whether you use prewritten or blank response cards, it is important to give students time to process the question, think of their response, place their response on the card, and finally display it for the teacher to see. Teachers can quickly monitor and adjust student learning by clearing up misconceptions, filling in learning gaps, or even using this as an opportunity to celebrate student on-target understandings.

Stop-n-Think Box 7.5

Identify the benefits and challenges of using choral responses and response cards in your classroom. Brainstorm ways to address the challenges.

Methods of Response	Benefits	Challenges	Address the Challenges
Choral responses			
Prewritten response cards			
Blank response cards			

Value Line-Up

Getting students to stand up, move to areas of the room that correspond with their answer, and then justify the response with classmates who are in the same location is an excellent way to foster active student responding. Let's look at one example. On one wall of the room, hang a sign that reads "Agree." On a different wall, hang a sign that reads "Strongly Agree." On the remaining two walls, hang the words "Disagree" and "Strongly Disagree." As the information is being shared with the students, have them place themselves on the continuum according to their opinion or prediction. The teacher should be prepared with several probing or clarifying questions that will give students the opportunity to elaborate on their position or engage in a moment of metacognition, both with their fellow voters and aloud to the entire class.

Again, the benefit of this strategy lies in the requirement that students think about and then justify their decision to classmates and the teacher. It goes without saying that the words on the walls can be whatever fits the lesson and are not limited to the preceding example.

Fill-In Notes

If you want students to stay engaged during a direct instruction lesson, do not give them a handout version of your PowerPoint or Keynote presentation. Instead, provide students with an outline with blanks to fill in. As you teach the lesson, students must fill in the notes. Students must actively listen to ensure that they are picking out the information that will complete their notes. Fill-in notes are most effective when teachers remove the major ideas and concepts from the outline. If you want students to think about what is important, make those terms blank in the fill-in notes.

At the end of a lesson or activity, allow students to compare fill-in notes to peer check or verify response. Finally, go over the notes with the entire class to ensure that everyone has the same answers.

Reading

Let's be honest. If you tell your students that you want them to read Chapter 10 for tomorrow, that translates into teenager speak as "no homework." However, teenagers must be able to read in order to learn. Reading material related to an experience in class or reading a section of the book prior to coming to class is absolutely vital to making learning a long-lasting experience (Howard, 2010a, 2010b). So how do we get teenagers to engage in reading and then connect what they read to science or mathematics class? The answer is that teachers must design and provide explicit strategies for teenage readers. Furthermore, these strategies must also be specifically targeted at the three phases of reading: prereading, during reading, and after reading.

Prereading

Strategies for prereading are designed to get students thinking about the content, making predictions, and activating prior knowledge. Prereading activities should be done at the end of class, before the reading is assigned for homework. These activities can be done individually or as a group. The goal is to give students a framework into which they will fit the content obtained from reading.

Prereading Strategies

1. Instruct students to quickly peruse the section or chapter and write down a brief summary of what they expect to gain from the reading.

2. Have students brainstorm what they already know about the topic presented in the section or chapter.

3. Make a list of key vocabulary that will be presented in the reading. Have students define the words or predict what they think the words mean.

4. Ask students to develop a list of questions about the content.

5. Look at the visuals or graphics in the section or chapter. Ask students to discuss and share any interesting visuals or graphics they discovered with a neighbor or the class. Have students respond to the following question: Why do you think the authors included this particular visual or graphic?

What other prereading strategies could you implement in your classroom?

Notice that the prereading activities are also strategies for activating prior knowledge. Simply put, strategies for activating prior knowledge are also effective when checking the level of student understanding. When using these prereading strategies, it is important to have students write down their thinking in their science notebooks, on a sheet of paper, or on poster paper to be revisited during and after reading.

During Reading

While students read text, it is absolutely vital for them to break the reading into segments (remember, we don't want too much too fast; it won't last). After each segment of the reading, students should stop and think about the reading to self-check for understanding or engage in an explicit activity designed by the teacher.

During-Reading Strategies

1. Have students complete fill-in notes as they read. This is often called a *reading guide*.

2. Have students stop after certain segments and write a summary about the information they just read.

3. Have students develop or complete a graphic organizer for each segment of the reading.

4. After reading a particular segment in class, have students turn to a neighbor and discuss the content. Share "aha" moments, surprises, or questions they may have.

5. As students come across answers to the prereading questions or vocabulary terms, they should edit and revise the prereading information to make sure it is accurate.

6. Engage your students in a focused reading. Ask them to make the following notations while reading:

   * next to something they want to remember,
   ! next to an essential piece of information,
   ✓ next to information that agrees with their thinking, and
   ? next to information that has raised a question.

These notations will also assist with follow-up discussions.

What other during-reading strategies could you implement in your classroom?

After Reading

Now that the reading is done, students need to do something with the information. In addition to answering the questions at the end of the section or chapter, students should create something with the reading content that relates to the class.

After-Reading Strategies

1. Develop an elevator speech about the major ideas, concepts, or topics from the reading.

2. Create a brochure or book cover that presents the information from the reading.

3. Develop a reading quiz and answer key to exchange with another student.

4. Create a graphic organizer for the reading.

5. Using the Cornell Notes template, create a set of notes for the reading.

6. Develop a game (e.g., Jeopardy, Taboo, $100,000 Pyramid, Who Wants to Be a Millionaire?) for the key vocabulary from the reading.

What other after-reading strategies can you think of to use in your classroom?

Notice that the after-reading activities are also strategies for creating novelty and establishing relevance. Again, novelty and relevance strategies are also effective as checks for understanding.

Helping our adolescent learners read to learn necessitates explicit strategies that require them to actively engage in the reading and continuously check for understanding.

Closure Activities

The class period ends in approximately seven minutes. You realize that you have not gotten through everything you had planned to get through. Furthermore, the homework assignment for the night requires the last segment of the lesson plan, which will not be done before the end of class. What do you do? Do you rush through the last bit of information quickly, letting the dismissal bell ring as you rapidly throw the content at your students? Or, do you stop, close the lesson with an exit activity, and cancel the homework?

> **Stop-n-Think Box 7.6**
>
> How do you structure the end of your classes? Are there particular activities or procedures you use to bring closure to your lessons?

I was sitting in a college education course many years ago when the professor told us a story about his two children. They were in his backyard on a beautiful summer afternoon attempting to catch butterflies. Like most stories, this story may remind you of a personal experience. For example, you may have immediately thought of catching lightning bugs, which was a favorite childhood experience. The professor explained that in a short time, his sons had caught more than half a dozen butterflies. Just about the time they were going to stop, the professor heard one of his sons crying: He had left the top off the container and all the butterflies had flown away. The professor paused for a moment and then said to the classroom full of future teachers, "I want you to close your eyes and picture my son sitting there and all the butterflies flying away over his head." He continued, saying, "Every time you decide not to do a closure activity at the end of your lesson, that is exactly what will happen to all the knowledge you just tried to put into your students' brains." Between the time your students leave your class and the time they return to the next class, most the information will have flown away. Hold on to that image.

Closure is a check for understanding that aids in the retention of student learning (Marzano, 2007). Keep in mind that closure is not about the teacher; it provides valuable time for the student to process information. It is not about the teacher getting up in front of the class and summarizing the learning outcomes, nor is it about the teacher reviewing the essential understandings. Closure is a mental process whereby the learner reflects on and summarizes what has been learned. The key focus here is the *learner* does the reflecting. The learner must engage in activities that ask him or her to state, summarize, verbalize, or express the learning. Closure can take many forms, whether verbal, written, or illustrated. The medium does not matter as long as it is an overt behavior that is completed by the student. Closure activities are needed whenever your students' brains require an opportunity to consolidate, organize, or summarize what has been learned to promote memory retention (Rasch & Born, 2007; Wang & Morris, 2010). As the teacher engages the students in a closure activity, he or she cues the students to the fact that they have arrived at an important point in the lesson and it is time to check their understanding and begin to internalize their thoughts. Closure provides an opportunity to reinforce the major points being learned by forming a coherent picture, which helps to eliminate rough drafts (Morris, 2006; Rasch & Born, 2007; Wang & Morris, 2010). It is not a matter of asking the students, "Do you have any questions?" but an opportunity to explicitly engage the major content.

Stop-n-Think Box 7.7

How do you check for understanding? What methods do you use to see whether your students are processing the information correctly?

As a teacher gathers information from the closure to make instructional decisions, it is essential that this information be visible, monitored, and measured. Checks for understanding are most effective when they utilize strategies that elicit an observable form of student thinking. The student must develop and then share his or her thinking in an overt manner that aligns directly with learning objectives. The process of developing and sharing a response in a clear and effective manner requires recall and then recoding of the information to complete the check for understanding. This exercise accomplishes two very important goals of the check: (1) the exercise reveals current rough drafts or gaps in student understanding, and (2) the exercise alone fills in rough drafts as students think about the ideas, concepts, or topics (Jensen, 2005; Medina et al., 2008; Morris, 2006; Rasch & Born, 2007). Therefore, the responses must be checked. Teachers must examine and analyze student responses in order to identify what has been learned, see possible gaps in the students' knowledge, and gather insight that will be used to provide the students with meaningful feedback. If these components are done effectively, not only will teachers improve their ability to monitor and adjust their instruction, but they will also be putting structures in place that actually hold students accountable for thinking about their learning.

Checking for understanding should be a routine, not an occasional occurrence. These checks are one type of formative assessment. The role of formative assessment or checks for understanding is well documented in the literature (Black & Wiliam, 1998; Hattie, 2009, 2012). The more times a check for understanding is implemented in the activity or lesson, the higher student achievement climbs (see Figure 7.2; Black & Wiliam, 1998; Hattie, 2009, 2012; Marzano, 2007).

On a regular basis (remember, "too much too fast, it won't last"), teachers must stop to find out whether students are mentally on the same page. As science and mathematics teachers, we continually emphasize the importance of developing a conceptual understanding

Figure 7.2   Effect Size Associated With the Number of Checks for Understanding Over 15 Weeks

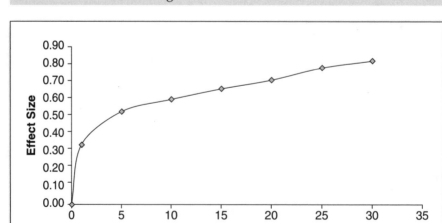

Source: Adapted from Bangert-Drowns, Kulik, and Kulik (1991).

of the ideas taught in our classrooms. As our science and mathematics assessments become more rigorous, checks for understanding become increasingly more important, so that teachers must be aware of whether or not their students have a conceptual understanding of classroom content. This can only happen if the teacher spends the necessary time to implement overt methods of checking for understanding.

Stop-n-Think Box 7.8

Brainstorm a list of reasons why so many teachers either avoid or eliminate the checking process. What are the barriers to successful implementation? List as many reasons as you can.

The list you developed in Stop-n-Think Box 7.8 probably includes "lack of time." Most teachers view the checking process as time consuming and a planning challenge. However, if we don't check, ultimately we will waste a lot of time reteaching later.

Meet Mr. Cooper

Mr. Cooper teachers eighth-grade pre-algebra. His class is working hard to understand the relationships between vertical, adjacent, complementary, and supplementary angles. Mr. Cooper asks the class whether they have any questions concerning the information he just presented. As several students nod their heads, it appears they are in agreement and understand his instruction. He assigns what he thinks is a simple worksheet for homework.

The following day he is quite surprised when many of the students report having extreme difficulty completing the homework. Looking at their work and answers on the worksheet, not to mention the number of students who did not complete the assignment, Mr. Cooper realizes there is an obvious gap in student learning. Most students did not finish and completed much of the worksheet incorrectly. In addition, Mr. Cooper's decision to not implement checks for understanding leaves him truly unsure of where the breakdown occurred.

To make matters worse, many of the students have practiced the concept incorrectly. The students were asked to complete an independent practice activity without being given opportunities to participate in guided practice. Unfortunately, the only outcome of Mr. Cooper's lesson on vertical, adjacent, complementary, and supplementary angles is a group of disengaged students who practiced a mathematics skill incorrectly over and over again.

A Watched Pot Never Boils . . . and This Is a Good Thing

As the saying goes, a watched pot never boils. In the kitchen, this is a maxim that is without any scientific validity, yet it still seems to be the case each time you want water to boil. Standing there watching the pot really does seem to prevent the liquid from boiling. When it comes to student learning, making sure it does not "boil" is exactly what you want to do. You do not want frustration, anxiety, and disengagement to boil over in the classroom, on the school bus, or at the dinner table. If these negative outcomes happen to boil over, there will be a mess that takes time to clean up. The mess, in this case, is a gap in student learning and a decrease in student engagement. In the classroom, watch the pot carefully. Monitor everything about the pot. Much like putting together a from-scratch, home-cooked meal, success takes time and careful monitoring. As teachers, if we turn a blind eye to our students' learning progress, the result will be as distasteful as undercooked chicken; dried-up macaroni and cheese; and unseasoned, overcooked green beans. The last step in the recipe for engagement is checking often for level of doneness, and by "doneness" we meaning learning.

CHAPTER 7: EXIT TICKET

Using the information from the chapter, fill in the following chart as a way to check your understanding.

Photo from
Thinkstock.com.

Brain Rule	The Brain Science Behind the Rule	Strategies for Addressing This in the Classroom
Learning takes time.		
Initial learning is fragile.		
Our brain creates rough drafts.		
What the brain thinks about it remembers.		

Engaging Professional Development Tasks

1. This professional development task develops a list of strategies that check for student understanding. Obtain a piece of poster paper and markers. Using the content and strategies presented in this chapter, develop a list of checks for understanding that are specific to your grade level or class. Hang this poster paper somewhere in your classroom so that you can easily see it while planning and teaching. Use this list of checks for under-standing as a prompt for everyday teaching.

2. This professional development task encourages the formation of connections between the previous chapters in the book. One noticeable characteristic of this particular chapter is that many of the strategies presented as checks for understanding were linked to previous ideas (i.e., activating prior knowledge, novelty, and relevance). On an 8½" × 11" sheet of paper, create a graphic organizer of the recipe and the strategies presented in this book. Add your own ideas and strategies as well. Share and discuss this graphic organizer with a colleague to help fill in

your rough draft of the recipe. Laminate it or put the graphic organizer in a sheet protector, and keep it available for your planning time. Use the graphic organizer as a motivator for developing engaging activities, lessons, and units.

References

Bangert-Drowns, R. L., Kulik, J. A., & Kulik, C. C. (1991). Effects of classroom testing. *Journal of Educational Research, 85*(2), 89–99.

Becker, W., & Carnine, D. (1980). Direct instruction: An effective approach for education intervention with the disadvantaged and low performers. In B. Lahey & A. Kazdin (Eds.), *Advances in child clinical psychology* (pp. 429–473). New York: Plenum.

Black, P., & Wiliam, D. (1998). Assessment and classroom learning. *Assessment in Education: Principles, Policy & Practice, 5*(1), 7–74.

Frankland, P. W., & Bontempi, B. (2005). The organization of recent and remote memories. *Nature Reviews Neuroscience, 6,* 119–130.

Gettinger, M., & Walter, M. J. (2012). Classroom strategies to enhance academic engaged time. In S. L. Christenson, A. L. Reschly, & C. Wylie (Eds.), *Handbook of research on student engagement Part 4* (pp. 653–673). New York: Springer.

Glickman, S. E. (1961). Perseverative neural processes and consolidation of the memory trace. *Psychological Bulletin, 58,* 218–233.

Hattie, J. A. C. (2009). *Visible learning. A synthesis of over 800 meta-analyses relating to achievement.* New York: Routledge.

Hattie, J. A. C. (2012). *Visible learning for teachers. Maximizing impact on learning.* New York: Routledge.

Howard, L. (2010a). *Five easy steps to a balanced science program for secondary grades.* Englewood, CO: Lead + Learn Press.

Howard, L. (2010b). *Five easy steps to a balanced science program for upper elementary and middle school grades.* Englewood, CO: Lead + Learn Press.

Hunter, M. (1982). *Master teaching.* El Segundo, CA: TIP.

Jensen, E. (2005). *Teaching with the brain in mind* (2nd ed.). Alexandria, VA: Association for Supervision and Curriculum Development.

Lewis, P. A., & Durrant, S. J. (2011). Overlapping memory replay during sleep builds cognitive schemata. *Trends in Cognitive Sciences, 15*(8), 343–351.

Loftus, E. F. (1979). The malleability of human memory: Information introduced after we view an incident can transform memory. *American Scientist, 67*(3), 312–320.

Marzano, R. J. (2007). *The art and science of teaching: A comprehensive framework for effective instruction.* Alexandria, VA: Association for Supervision and Curriculum Development.

McClelland, J. L., McNaughton, B. L., & O'Reilly, R. C. (1995). Why there are complementary learning systems in the hippocampus and neocortex: Insights from the successes and failures of connectionist models of learning and memory. *Psychological Review, 102,* 419–457.

McGaugh, J. L. (1966). Time-dependent processes in memory storage. *Science, 153*, 1351–1358.

McGaugh, J. L. (2000). Memory: A century of consolidation. *Science, 287*, 248–251.

McKenzie, G. (1979). Effects of questions and testlike events on achievement and on-task behavior in a classroom concept learning presentation. *Journal of Educational Research, 72*, 348–350.

McKenzie, G. R., & Henry, M. (1979). Effects of testlike events on on-task behavior, text anxiety, and achievement in a classroom rule-learning task. *Journal of Educational Psychology, 71*, 370–374.

Medina, J. H., Bekinschtein, P., Cammarota, M., & Izquierdo, I. (2008). Do memories consolidate to persist or do they persist to consolidate? *Behavioural Brain Research, 192*, 61–69.

Morris, R. G. (2006). Elements of a neurobiological theory of hippocampal function: The role of synaptic plasticity, synaptic tagging and schemas. *European Journal of Neuroscience, 23*, 2829–2846.

Polster, M. R., Nadel, L., & Schacter, D. L. (1991). Cognitive neuroscience analysis of memory: A historical perspective. *Journal of Cognitive Neuroscience, 3*(2), 95–116.

Rasch, B., & Born, J. (2007). Maintaining memories by reactivation. *Current Opinion in Neurobiology, 17*, 698–703.

Rosenshine, B., & Stevens, R. (1986). Teaching functions. In M. C. Whittrock (Ed.), *Third handbook of research on teaching* (3rd ed., pp. 376–391). New York: Macmillan.

Squire, L. R. (1992). Memory and the hippocampus: A synthesis from findings with rats, monkeys, and humans. *Psychological Review, 99*, 195–231.

Squire, L. R., & Alvarez, P. (1995). Retrograde amnesia and memory consolidation: A neurobiological perspective. *Current Opinion in Neurobiology, 5*, 169–177.

Squire, L. R., Cohen, N. J., & Nadel, L. (1984). The medial temporal region and memory consolidation: A new hypothesis. In H. Weingartner & E. S. Parker (Eds.), *Memory consolidation: Psychobiology of cognition* (pp. 185–210). Hillsdale, NJ: Lawrence Erlbaum Associates.

Takashima, A., Petersson, K. M., Rutters, F., Tendolkar, I., Jensen, O., Zwarts, M. J., . . . Fernandez, G. (2006). Declarative memory consolidation in humans: A prospective functional magnetic resonance imaging study. *Proceedings of the National Academy of Sciences of the United States of America, 103*(3), 756–761.

Tse, D., Takeuchi, T., Kakeyama, M., Kajii, Y., Okuno, H., Tohyama, C., . . . Morris, R. G. M. (2011). Schema-dependent gene activation and memory encoding in neocortex. *Science 333*, 891–895.

van Kesteren, M. T. R., Fernandez, G., Norris, D. G., & Hermans, E. J. (2010). Persistent schema-dependent hippocampal-neocortical connectivity during memory encoding and postencoding rest in humans. *Proceedings of the National Academy of Sciences, U.S.A., 107*, 7550–7555.

van Kesteren, M. T. R., Rijpkema, M., Ruiter, D. J., & Fernandez, G. (2010). Retrieval of associative information congruent with prior knowledge is related to increased medial prefrontal activity and connectivity. *Journal of Neuroscience, 30*, 15888–15894.

van Kesteren, M. T. R., Ruiter, D. J., Fernandez, G., & Henson, R. N. (2012). How schema and novelty augment memory formation. *Trends in Neuroscience, 35*(4), 211–219.

Wang, S. H., & Morris, R. G. (2010). Hippocampal-neocortical interactions in memory formation, consolidation, and reconsolidation. *Annual Review of Psychology, 61*, 49–79.

Willingham, D. T. (2009). *Why don't students like school? A cognitive scientist answers questions about how the mind works and what it means for the classroom.* San Francisco: Jossey-Bass.

Wiltgen, B. J., Brown, R. A. M., Talton, L. E., & Silva, A. J. (2004). New circuits for old memories: The role of the neocortex in consolidation. *Neuron, 44,* 101–108.

Wolfe, P. (2010). *Brain matters. Translating research into classroom practice* (2nd ed.). Alexandria, VA: Association for Supervision and Curriculum Development.

8

Building an Engaging Science or Mathematics Lesson and Unit

S o what's next? Now that the recipe for engagement has been quite thoroughly covered, putting it to use in a science or mathematics classroom is the next task. Let's review: The recipe for engaging science and mathematics students contains six "must-have" ingredients.

Photo from Thinkstock.com.

1. **Prime** the brain. Stir.

2. Sprinkle in the right amount of **novelty**. Continue to stir.

3. Insert a good portion of **relevance**. Blend together with the content often.

4. Pour into the **big picture** and mix together some more.

5. **Marinate** for approximately 15 minutes; then stir once more.

6. Allow to cook for two to three days, **checking** often for degree of doneness. Stir as needed.

Science and mathematics teachers can use this recipe as a framework for planning and developing their next lesson. Whether the topic is cell theory, simple circuits, erosion, natural resources, rational expressions, logarithmic functions, polynomials, quadrilaterals, or the power rule in calculus, engaging the student brain requires that the lesson primes the brain; incorporates novelty, relevance, the big picture, and the chunking of content; and checks for understanding.

The recipe for engaging the student brain also provides a framework for structuring your next unit on simple machines, weather, right triangle trigonometry, or probability. Does your unit have an explicit plan for activating and linking to prior knowledge? Does your unit have an engaging scenario that provides a concrete context for promoting behavioral relevance? Is the content in your next unit chunked into appropriate segments? Finally, how will you offer students the opportunity to check their level of understanding throughout the unit? What information will you collect to ensure students are developing mastery of the content?

Let's look at two planning templates and how they can guide the next steps in engaging the student brain: designing lesson plans and unit plans that engage the brain.

Using the Recipe to Build an Engaging Lesson

Let's start small. In other words, before trying to design a unit with the recipe, let's try it out with a single lesson plan. Figure 8.1 provides a guide to developing a lesson plan that incorporates each part of the recipe for engagement.

Figure 8.1   Daily Lesson Plan

Content/Topic: _____

Standard(s)	Materials

Objective(s): (What the students will know, understand, and be able to do)

Checks for Understanding: (A list of possible checks for understandings aligned with the objectives and standards for this lesson.)

Lesson Component	Possible Strategies, Examples	Probable Outcomes
Opening activity or event	discrepant events, engaging scenario, video clips, movement, stories, flexible groupings	motivation, meaningful connections, generate curiosity, emotional hooks, build background knowledge, novelty, synergy
Activation of prior knowledge	KWL, brainstorming, mind mapping, a turn-to, questioning, prereading, graphic organizers, metaphors and analogies, interest inventories, similarities and differences	"aha" moments, relevance, meaningful connections, increase rate and degree of learning, understand relationship among and between concepts

(Continued)

Figure 8.1 (Continued)

Lesson Component	Possible Strategies, Examples	Probable Outcomes
Learning segment or chunk 1	direct instruction, essential questions, big picture (that you will pour content into during the lesson), jigsaw, teacher modeling	establish foundation, stimulate purpose, novelty, guided practice
Check for understanding 1	choral response, response cards, value line up, write a summary, peer conferencing and teaching	increased retention, students understand the criteria for success, metacognition, active participation, simultaneous interactions
Learning segments followed by checks for understanding is a continuous learning cycle until all learning "chunks" for the lesson have been completed. Remember: Teach 10 to 12 minutes and follow that learning session with an opportunity for students to process the knowledge (check for understanding).		
Closure activity	This activity is designed to provide an opportunity for students to recode and consolidate the learning. This activity should enable students to fit the content of the lesson into the big picture by referencing the essential questions for the unit.	
	summarizing activity (write your principal an e-mail, etc.) journaling, 3-2-1, $100,000 Pyramid, wage a bet, turn-to, independent practice, exit ticket	increased retention, graphic organizers, recall, moving information from short-term to long-term memory
Homework	independent practice, reflective tasks, creating linguistic and nonlinguistic representations of material presented, learning menus, metacognitive activities	increased retention, identification of gaps and misunderstandings, establish ownership over learning, individual accountability Homework can be used to set the stage for tomorrow's instruction.

Post-Instruction

Self-Reflection

Ask yourself the following questions:

- As you engaged students in your check for understanding activities, what did the student responses tell you about their level of understanding?
- What gaps or misconceptions did your students have about the material?
- What adjustments need to be made in the future?
- Reflect on the closure activity: Were the students able to articulate the content from the lesson? Did the students understand the connection to the big picture?
- Are the students able to answers the essential questions?

Stop-n-Think Box 8.1

Brainstorm how you would complete the Figure 8.1 template for an upcoming lesson that you will be teaching. What activities will you select?

Using the Recipe to Build an Engaging Unit

Figure 8.2 provides a guide to developing a unit plan that incorporates each part of the recipe for engagement.

Stop-n-Think Box 8.2

Brainstorm how Figure 8.2 would look for an upcoming unit that you will be teaching. How will you map out this unit into individual lessons?

Keep in mind that each template includes each component of the recipe. This is important. Focusing on only one step or excluding a step because of lack of time is not going to provide the same outcomes. Simply making learning novel without "checking for degree of doneness" does not do the student brain any favors, just like a teaspoon of salt, a necessity in any cookie recipe, is never as delectable by itself as in freshly baked chocolate chip cookies. Together the ingredients create a classroom environment that will not only increase

Figure 8.2 Unit Instructional Plan

Theme/Topic: _____

Key Ideas and Concepts	Standards
A list of nouns from the standards addressed in this unit.	Include the complete standards and substandards for this unit.

Essential Questions

Three or four guiding questions for this unit.

Engaging Scenario

Using the nouns extracted from the standards, develop an authentic context for the unit and a series of performance tasks.

Learning Progression (Map out the progression of topics for the unit.)

Develop a visual or graphic organizer of the progression of topics for this unit. Include an estimate of the time spent on each topic.

Resources Needed	To Do List
Leveled books, reference materials, technology, laboratory materials, websites, etc.	Things to be done before the start of the unit.

student engagement in the learning experience; it will ultimately increase the level of student achievement in your classroom.

A Recipe for Diversity

What about science or mathematics students who are simply unmotivated? You are likely to have students who have a learning disability or experience attention problems in your classroom. What about those learners who are not native speakers of English and do not have the academic vocabulary of other students? How do you engage students who are gifted and have mastered much of the curriculum or acquire the content at a much more rapid pace?

How to address the individual needs of the wide range of learners who populate your science or mathematics class would take volumes, not chapters, to discuss. However, a brief look at how the recipe in this book can be easily adjusted to meet the needs of diverse learners will help jump start our thinking about the recipe as an approach that truly engages all learners in science and mathematics.

Learned Helplessness or Unmotivated Learners

Student A is in fourth-period algebra and seems to be simply unmotivated. This is his second time through the course. As he sits in his seat, Student A appears edgy. On some days, he sits at his desk in a trance-like state and does not snap out of it quickly. During most activities in algebra, this student appears bored and disconnected. He is not very good at prioritizing tasks and makes careless mistakes on most assignments. Over time, he has isolated himself from the rest of the class and has decreased social contact. He is absent due to illness much more often than his peers.

Student A suffers from learned helplessness, a behavioral condition that stems from individuals feeling as if they have no control over a negative outcome. Students who experience chronic failure eventually throw up their hands, withdraw, and fail to see any possible outcome other than a negative outcome. Unfortunately, this is common in the science classroom and even more familiar in a mathematics classroom (Maier & Seligman, 1976; Maier & Watkins, 2005).

Stop-n-Think Box 8.3

How would the recipe need to be adjusted for a student who experiences learned helplessness?

Students experiencing learned helplessness respond best to adjustments in their classroom environment that promote positive and successful interactions with their teacher and peers. For example, these students need more physical activity, more positive emotional engagement, goal setting, and increased checks for understanding. Thus, the recipe would be heavy on novelty to induce more positive emotionally charged events, energizers to stimulate the brain, and more personalized attention with regard to feedback and monitoring progress toward specific goals. Teachers should break down big goals into smaller, more manageable chunks so that the student can begin to experience immediate success. Celebrate that success and make it an emotionally charged event. Furthermore, these students need the classroom environment to be behaviorally relevant and safe, to eliminate the threat of yet another public failure. Help these students feel successful and a part of an engaging classroom (Jensen, 2010).

Learning Disabilities

For students with a learning disability, the frustrations of inconsistent performance across academic areas are exacerbated by feelings linked to slowed problem-solving skills, impaired perceptions, difficulty generalizing information, visual-spatial deficits, weaker cognition, impaired concept formation, and slowed abstract reading. As research provides better data and information on interventions that target general and specific learning disabilities, more evidence-based practices are available to classroom teachers. These strategies and the components of the recipe will help prevent vulnerable students from falling through the cracks by providing them with a more engaging, enriching, and student-centered learning environment (Raymond, 2012).

Stop-n-Think Box 8.4

How would the recipe need to be adjusted for a student who has a learning disability?

The recipe for a student with a learning disability will be heavy on building and activating background knowledge. Strategies that build background knowledge through a variety of activities using different modalities will help these students build a foundation for learning that may not happen as naturally as with their peers (Raymond, 2012; Vaughn & Bos, 2011). The chunking of directions, information, and tasks into smaller pieces helps the brain conserve the energy needed to take on multistep events and focus that energy on concept development and attainment. Equally important is an emphasis on concrete experiences. Extra attention on checks for understanding that promote recall and retention will provide opportunities for multiple exposures to content and provide the support for long-lasting learning by affirming the student's progress (Vaughn & Bos, 2011). Finally, the use of novelty to get the learner's attention and promote positive emotional experiences will trigger motivation and meaningful connections (Raymond, 2012).

Attention-Deficit/Hyperactivity Disorder

Student B is a student in a high school earth science class. She rushes into tasks, rarely finishing them; demands constant attention; is often moody, disorganized, and spacey; displays poor short-term memory; has difficulty following directions; commonly is late for deadlines; has poor concentration; does not seem to have the ability to plan ahead; and is poor at reflecting on the past. She seems to always want to be in motion and is forever trying to do several things at once. Student B has every possible symptom of attention-deficit/hyperactivity disorder (Jensen, 2010).

> ### Stop-n-Think Box 8.5
>
> How would the recipe need to be adjusted for a student with attention-deficit/hyperactivity disorder?

Suggestions should target adjusting the levels of novelty, examining the size of the learning chunks, and increasing the number of checks for understanding. Students who live with the symptoms of an attention disorder often have underperforming brains (Castellanos & Acosta, 2004; Kieling, Goncalves, Tannock, & Castellanos, 2008). The brain's regions that manage attention are functioning below normal levels and thus need to be awakened (Kieling et al., 2008). Therefore, you need to energize the science or mathematics classroom with novelty and activities that are behaviorally relevant. Furthermore, develop checks for understanding that include cooperative learning strategies (e.g., study buddies); to-do lists; writing steps down for future reference; explicit instruction of note-taking strategies; time for extra reflection and processing; and aid in identifying important ideas, concepts, or topics. Teachers should also consider helping the student's working memory by clarifying and repeating instructions or providing him or her with a visual representation of the directions. Breaking tasks and information into smaller chunks will also help the hippocampus process the relevant stimuli.

English-Language Learners

Approximately 20% of school-age children in the United States are English-language learners, and 14% to 16% of those students speak Spanish (Carrillo-Syrja, 2012). One of the most significant challenges that these students face is the lack of academic vocabulary needed to successfully master complex learning (Marzano, 2004).

Stop-n-Think Box 8.6

How would the recipe need to be adjusted for a student who is an English-language learner?

For this type of learner, targeted strategies for building background knowledge and linking new learning to prior knowledge are paramount. Given the importance of vocabulary knowledge, these students need to experience novel, repeated exposures to vocabulary in the form of games, nonlinguistic formats, and concrete experiences. Furthermore, the pace at which the direct instruction of vocabulary is presented should be monitored to ensure that they do not get "too much, too fast" in terms of new words and concepts. The recipe should be front loaded to help keep these students engaged.

Gifted Students

Student C is an eleventh grader enrolled in both pre-calculus and physics. Student C demonstrates general and specific academic abilities well above average for a young man his age. Furthermore, he demonstrates hyperfocus on specific tasks and has incredible creativity (Renzulli, 1986). As a result, he acquires knowledge at an incredible pace and easily uses that knowledge to create new products or form new ideas. However, left alone without an engaging classroom environment to quench his thirst for learning, Student C could easily disengage and become an under-achieving gifted student.

> ### Stop-n-Think Box 8.7
>
> How would the recipe need to be adjusted for a student who is gifted?

Much like the recipe for the previous students, the recipe for gifted children will need some adjusting. Once the teacher has identified the depth and breadth of a gifted student's background knowledge, designing instruction that is novel and relevant to his or her interests and ability level is very important. Students who acquire the core content quickly should be encouraged to develop products and ideas that extend this core content. Science and mathematics classrooms that move too slowly for gifted students are disengaging. Gifted students need the freedom to move along at a pace that aligns with the speed at which they acquire knowledge. As these students wrestle with complex ideas, they can often take on larger chunks of information, as long as it is both novel and relevant. Furthermore, these students benefit from explicit instruction on how to self-monitor through individualized checks for understanding. To keep them engaged, ramp up the recipe with choice and metacognition.

Taste Testing the Recipe

The recipe will look different for different learners. If you know your students and understand their individual needs, you can adjust the recipe to move your science or mathematics classroom one step closer to engaging all learners. Strategies such as tiered assignments, compacting, flexible grouping, or sponge activities for students who finish a task early help differentiate within an engaging classroom (Gregory & Chapman, 2008; Gregory & Hammerman, 2008; Tomlinson, 1999, 2001). Each one of the learners described earlier will thrive in a more engaging classroom that meets his or her individual needs. What is unique about each of the situations described earlier is that the emphasis is placed on different parts of the recipe, depending on the individual needs of the learner. That is, adjust the recipe to taste!

An engaging science and mathematics class

1. provides opportunities for students to dig up and activate prior knowledge;

2. encourages students to make meaning of their prior knowledge and explicitly link it to new learning;

3. engages students in activities that build background knowledge through active learning if prior knowledge is weak;

4. uses novel experiences like discrepant events that capture the students' attention and excite them about ideas, concepts, and topics;

5. incorporates music and movement to evoke positive emotionally charged events;

6. uses strategies that are behaviorally relevant to the student because they provide essential questions, student choice, engaging scenarios, and inconsequential competition;

7. encourages students to ask questions, make mistakes, and to take risks in a safe environment;

8. enables students to see the big picture for learning;

9. provides students with opportunities to stop, process, and reflect on their learning, to avoid flooding the brain with too much input;

10. includes continual checks for understanding that encourage students to recall and review content;

11. includes continual checks for understanding that provide data to the classroom teacher about the learning progress of his or her students; and

12. leaves students on the edge of their seats wanting more.

Steve Spangler of Steve Spangler Science (http://www.steve spanglerscience.com) says that if what you did in your classroom that day makes it to the dinner table, you win! As science and mathematics teachers, we want to win every day. Using the recipe to whip up an engaging science or mathematics class gives us the best chance of our lesson making it to the dinner table and the best chance for our students to achieve. The next step is to develop your personal action plan and implement the ideas presented in this book. Good luck!

CHAPTER 8: EXIT TICKET

Develop a Personal Action Plan

Given what I now know about the engaging the brain, what will I do next or do differently in my classroom?

Photo from Thinkstock.com.

Where will I look for support in implementing these ideas?

Engaging Professional Development Tasks

1. This professional development task combines the concepts presented in this book with the lesson planning process. Start small. Using the template in Figure 8.1, create a lesson that incorporates one or two ideas from the book. Implement the lesson plan in an upcoming class. Afterward, reflect on the experience.

2. After completing the first lesson plan, create a second lesson plan and incorporate one or two different ideas from the book. Again, implement and reflect. Continue this process, trying out one or two different strategies each time.

3. This professional development task combines the concepts presented in this book with the unit planning process. Once you have gotten comfortable with individual ideas or strategies presented in the book, use the Figure 8.2 template to map out an instructional unit on an upcoming topic. Keep a reflection journal of the unit to provide insight and suggestions for planning the next unit or for planning the same unit next semester or year.

References

Carrillo-Syrja, R. (2012). *Common formative assessments for English language learners.* Englewood, CO: Lead + Learn Press.

Castellanos, F. X., & Acosta, M. T. (2004). The neuroanatomy of attention deficit-hyperactivity disorder. *Revista de Neurologia, 38*(Suppl. 1), S131–S136.

Gregory, G., & Chapman, C. (2008). *Differentiated instructional strategies. One size doesn't fit all* (2nd ed.). Thousand Oaks, CA: Corwin.

Gregory, G., & Hammerman, E. (2008). *Differentiated instructional strategies for science grades K-8.* Thousand Oaks, CA: Corwin.

Jensen, E. P. (2010). *Different brains, different learners: How to reach the hard to reach* (2nd ed.). Alexandria, VA: Association for Supervision and Curriculum Development.

Kieling, C., Goncalves, R. R., Tannock, R., & Castellanos, F. X. (2008). Neurobiology of attention deficit-hyperactivity disorder. *Child and Adolescent Psychiatric Clinics of North America, 17*(2), 285–307.

Maier, S. F., & Seligman, M. E. P. (1976). Learned helplessness: Theory and evidence. *Journal of Experimental Psychology: General, 105,* 3–46.

Maier, S. F., & Watkins, L. R. (2005). Stressor controllability and learned helplessness: The roles of the dorsal raphe nucleus, serotonin, and corticotropin-releasing factor. *Neuroscience and Biobehavioral Reviews, 29,* 829–841.

Marzano, R. J. (2004). *Building background knowledge for academic achievement. Research on what works in schools.* Alexandria, VA: Association for Supervision and Curriculum Development.

Raymond, E. B. (2012). *Learners with mild disabilities: A characteristics approach* (4th ed.). Boston: Pearson Education.

Renzulli, J. S. (1986). The three-ring conception of giftedness: A developmental model for creative productivity. In R. J. Sternberg & J. E. Davidson (Eds.), *Conceptions of giftedness* (pp. 53–92). New York: Cambridge University Press.

Tomlinson, C. A. (1999). *The differentiated classroom. Responding to the needs of all learners.* Alexandria, VA: Association for Supervision and Curriculum Development.

Tomlinson, C. A. (2001). *How to differentiate instruction in mixed-ability classrooms* (2nd ed.). Alexandria, VA: Association for Supervision and Curriculum Development.

Vaughn, S. R., & Bos, C. S. (2011). *Strategies for teaching students with learning and behavior problems* (8th ed.). Upper Saddle River, NJ: Prentice Hall.

Appendix A

Unit Instructional Plan

Topic: _____

Key Ideas, Concepts, and Ideas	Standards

(Continued)

(Continued)

Essential Questions

Engaging Scenario

Learning Progression (Map out the progression of topics for the unit.)

Resources Needed	To-Do List

Appendix B

Daily Lesson Plan

Topic: _____

Standard	Supplies

Objective(s) for the Lesson:	
Checks for Understanding:	

Component	Detailed Description
Opening Activity or Event	

Component	Detailed Description
Activation of Prior Knowledge	
Learning Segment or Chunk 1	
Check for Understanding 1	
Learning Segment or Chunk 2	
Check for Understanding 2	
Learning Segment or Chunk 3	
Check for Understanding 3	
Closure Activity	
Homework:	

Post-Instruction

Reflections From the Checks for Understanding:

Reflections From the Closure Activity:

Things to Keep in Mind for the Next Class:

Index

CORWIN
A SAGE Company

The Corwin logo—a raven striding across an open book—represents the union of courage and learning. Corwin is committed to improving education for all learners by publishing books and other professional development resources for those serving the field of PreK–12 education. By providing practical, hands-on materials, Corwin continues to carry out the promise of its motto: **"Helping Educators Do Their Work Better."**